Tax Facts 11

Tax Facts 11

BY JOEL EMES *AND* MICHAEL WALKER

The Fraser Institute

Vancouver   British Columbia   Canada

1999

Printed in Canada.

Canadian Cataloguing in Publication Data

Emes, Joel, 1968
 Tax Facts 11

 Includes bibliographical references.
 ISBN 0-88975-192-7

 1. Taxation--Canada. 2. Tax incidence--Canada. I. Walker, Michael, 1945- II. Fraser Institute (Vancouver, B.C.) III. Title. IV. Title: Tax facts eleven.

HJ2449.E43 1999   336.2'00971   C99-910177-3

Contents

Tables and Figures

Tables

iv

Figures

About the Authors

JOEL EMES is a research economist at The Fraser Institute. He is a regular contributor to the Fraser Institute's monthly magazine *Fraser Forum*, and co-author of *Tax Facts 10* and *Canada's All Government Debt (1996 edition)*. His articles have appeared in the *Globe and Mail*, the *Calgary Herald*, and the *London Free Press*. Mr. Emes is also the primary researcher for Tax Freedom Day and the Institute's Provincial and State-Provincial fiscal comparisons, the Budget Performance Index and the Fiscal Performance Index. He received his M.A. in Economics from Simon Fraser University in 1995.

MICHAEL WALKER is an economist, journalist, broadcaster, consultant, university lecturer, and public speaker. As an economist, he has written or edited 40 books on economic topics. His articles on technical economic subjects have appeared in professional journals in Canada, the United States, and Europe, including the *Canadian Journal of Economics*, the *American Economic Review, The Journal of Finance*, the *Canadian Tax Journal, Health Management Quarterly*, and *Health Affairs*. As a journalist, he has written over 675 articles, which have appeared in some 60 newspapers, including the *Globe and Mail*, the *Wall Street Journal*, the *Vancouver Sun*, the *Chicago Tribune*, the *Reader's Digest*, the *Detroit News* and the *Western Star*—the newspaper in his birthplace, Corner Brook, Newfoundland. Dr Walker has been a regular columnist in the *Vancouver Province*, the *Toronto Sun*, and the *Ottawa Citizen*; he is also a member of The *Financial Post* Board of Economists. As a broadcaster, he has written and delivered some 2,000 radio broadcasts on economic topics and appeared on radio and television programs in Canada, the United States, and Latin America. As a consultant, he has provided advice to private groups and governments in the United States, Argentina, Australia, Bermuda, Brazil, Chile, Hong Kong, Jamaica, New Zealand, Mexico, Panama, Peru, Sweden, Venezuela, and Canada. He has lectured to over 1,000 audiences at universities and in other venues on five continents.

Since 1974, Michael Walker has directed the activities of the Fraser Institute. Before that, he taught at the University of Western Ontario and Carleton University and was employed at the Bank of Canada and the Federal Department of Finance. He received his Ph.D. at the University of Western Ontario and his B.A. at St. Francis Xavier University.

He is a director of a number of firms and other enterprises, including The Mont Pelerin Society, Mancal Corporation, The Milton and Rose D. Friedman Foundation, The Max Bell Foundation, Canada-Ukraine Chamber of Commerce, and Hollyburn Country Club. He is also a member of the Editorial Consultative Committee of the Development Research Centre Institute of the State Council, People's Republic of China. In 1992, he was awarded the Colin M. Brown Freedom Medal by the National Citizens Coalition.

Acknowledgments

We are pleased to acknowledge the assistance of Statistics Canada which provided certain unpublished background data essential to this study. The Canadian Tax Simulator computer programs were originally written by David Gill whose unsparing efforts we are pleased to acknowledge.

The sixth and seventh editions were computed on a set of programs modified to run on a microcomputer system. These modifications were completed by Douglas T. Wills.

The eighth, ninth and tenth editions of *Tax Facts* were computed using the SPSS statistical package with programming provided by Filip Palda and Isabella Horry.

Disclaimer

A portion of this analysis is based on Statistics Canada's Social Policy Simulation Database and Model. The assumptions and calculations underlying the simulation results were prepared by the authors and the responsibility for the use and interpretation of these data is entirely theirs.

Preface

This book is a summary of the latest results of a Fraser Institute project that began in July, 1975. Its objective was to find out how much tax, in all forms, Canadians pay to federal, provincial, and municipal governments and how the size of this tax bill has changed over the years since 1961. In the interim, ten editions of this book have been published.

The book has been written with two distinct purposes in mind: first, to provide a non-technical do-it-yourself manual so that the average Canadian family can estimate how much tax it pays; and second, to update a statistic, first published in 1976, that we call the Canadian Consumer Tax Index. This index measures how much the tax bill of an average Canadian family has increased since 1961 and by how much it is changing currently. In other words, it measures changes in the price that Canadians pay for government.

This book does not attempt to look at the benefits that Canadians receive from government in return for their taxes. Rather, it looks at the price that is paid for a product—government. It has nothing to say about the quality of the product, how much of it each of us receives, or whether we get our money's worth. These questions are, however, considered in various Fraser Institute publications, including *Government Spending Facts 2*, and our government report cards.

Many of the recent statistics contained in this book are based on output from Statistics Canada's Social Policy Simulation Database and Model (SPSD/M), a microsimulation model of the Canadian tax and transfer system. Prior to 1992, the analysis was done with group average data pre-compiled by Statistics Canada. Because the analysis is now built up from families, it is possible to examine the situation of particular types of taxpayers with a good deal more precision.

The Fraser Institute calculations of the tax burden are part of an on-going program of research. In making these results available to the public we seek both to inform and to be informed. Readers who disagree with our methods or conclusions are invited to write to the Institute to convey the nature of their reservations. In this way, our methods and our estimates can be refined and perfected.

—Michael A. Walker

Tax Facts 11

Chapter 1
The Canadian Tax System

Undoubtedly, one of the most unpopular policies in Canadian history was the introduction of the Goods and Services Tax (GST) in 1991. In part, its political unpopularity was due to the fact that many Canadians thought that this was a new tax that would increase the tax burden. But, it also reflected a deep-seated concern on the part of citizens about the process of government, and revealed the belief held by many that the government was collecting too many tax dollars while accomplishing too little in the way of public services.

The most significant revelation in the reaction to the GST, however, was that the Canadian public has very little real information about the tax system. Very few knew that the GST was replacing a tax already in place and fewer still realized that the federal government's main ambition was not to raise more revenue but rather to replace the Manufacturers' Tax. Everyone who had studied the Manufacturers' Tax had concluded that it was a terrible tax that had many unintended negative effects. It was a tax that had to be replaced but Canadians' ignorance about it was a significant barrier to its removal. While some would say that there is no such thing as a good tax, it is the case that, as long as there is a demand for public expenditures, there will have to be taxes to finance them. We now know that taxes distort people's decisions, leaving opportunities for mutually beneficial exchanges unexploited. The task, then, is to design an efficient set of taxes, one that does not unduly interfere with the types of decisions people make in the marketplace.

There is, then, something worse than a tax and that is a badly designed tax, which, in addition to taking spending power from the private sector, also distorts everyday decisions in a way that is neither desirable nor necessary. As free international trade becomes a reality, it is increasingly important that governments implement efficient and sensibly designed tax systems. A prerequisite to being able to debate and design such taxes is a base of information about them. The purpose of this book is to provide a basic tool kit of knowledge about taxation in Canada in order to enhance the opportunity for rational debate about these issues.

This book is an important resource for everyone concerned about the extent and relatively rapid growth of taxation in this country. Between 1981 and 1998, the total tax bill of the average Canadian family from all three levels of government increased in real terms by $4,233 in 1998 dollars. Figure 1.1 charts the progress of taxes for selected years since 1981.

The many faces of the tax collector

The Canadian tax system is continually changing. To understand current developments it is important to know how the Canadian taxation system has evolved. Under the Canadian Constitution, the federal and provincial governments are essentially given unlimited powers of taxation. Under the *British North America Act*, the immediate predecessor of the Canadian Constitution, the federal parliament has the power to raise money by any mode or system of taxation while the provinces are limited to collecting taxes that are paid directly by the person being taxed—so-called direct taxes. But, because of the broad judicial interpretation of the meaning of the word "direct," the provinces have been able to levy all sorts of taxes, except for import duties and taxes on sales that cross provincial borders. Given this unlimited scope for taxation and more than 125 years of ingenuity, it is not surprising that Canada now has a very complicated tax system. See Lewis 1978 for a survey of the Canadian tax system's evolution with emphasis on the sharing of tax revenues between the provinces and the federal government.

To begin to understand some of this complexity, look at the 29 categories of tax set out in figure 1.2 and consider how rebates, reductions, allowances, credits, abatements, and surcharges affect the tax bills of Canadians.

Income taxes predominate

Table 1.1 and figure 1.3 show that personal income taxes are the largest single source of government revenue. During 1997, some $114 billion was extracted by federal and provincial income tax—a sum that represented 39.3 percent of the total taxes that Canadians pay. Second in line as a source of federal and provincial revenues was the sales tax—representing 14.8 percent of tax revenue and 43 billion tax dollars. Taxes on

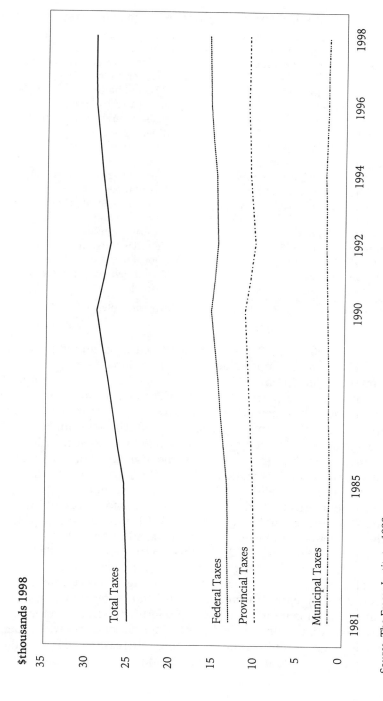

Figure 1.1: Federal, Provincial, and Municipal Taxes Collected from the Average Canadian Family, 1981-1998, ($1998)

Source: The Fraser Institute, 1998.

Figure 1.2: Revenue Sources Used in Determining Equalization Payments

Personal income taxes	Mined oil revenues
Business income revenues	Domestically sold natural
Capital tax revenues	gas revenues
General and miscellaneous	Exported natural gas revenues
sales taxes	Sale of Crown leases
Tobacco taxes	Other oil and gas revenues
Gasoline revenue	Mineral resources:
Diesel fuel revenue	asbestos, coal, other
Non-commercial vehicle licenses	Potash revenues
Commercial vehicle licences	Water power rentals
Alcoholic beverage revenues	Payroll taxes
Hospital and medical insurance	Provincial—local property
premiums	tax revenues
Race track taxes	Lottery revenues
Forestry revenues	Miscellaneous provincial—
NORP oil revenues	local taxes and revenues
Old oil revenues	Shared revenues: preferred share
Heavy oil revenues	dividend

Source: Canadian Tax Foundation, *Finances of the Nation*, 1997, table 8.5.

corporate profits, at 9.3 percent of total taxes, accounted for a further $27 billion, while property and natural resource taxes combined accounted for $35 billion, or 12.2 percent. Together, these five kinds of tax accounted for 75.5 percent of total government revenue during 1997. Almost one-half of government tax revenue comes from personal income tax and the corporate profits tax, which were implemented in 1916 and 1917 as "temporary" measures to finance World War I.

Table 1.1 also illustrates how the Canadian tax structure has evolved over the 37 years since 1961. The most obvious change has been the increased reliance on the personal income tax. While always a prominent feature of the tax system, the income tax has in recent years become even more important. In 1961, income taxes represented only 22.7 cents out of every tax dollar Canadians paid but by 1997 income taxes accounted for 39.3 cents—over two-and-a-half times the revenue generated by the next largest source, sales taxes.

This increase came about largely through passive interaction between the progressive income tax system and money incomes swollen by inflation. This interaction is often referred to as "bracket creep" because taxpayers can be pushed into higher tax brackets when their income goes up to compensate them for an increase in the general price level. Until the income tax system was indexed to the inflation rate in

Table 1.1: Taxes Paid and Percent of Total Taxes, 1961 and 1997

| | 1961 | | 1997 | |
	$millions	percent	$millions	percent
Personal income tax	2,099	22.7	113,789	39.3
General sales tax	1,351	14.6	42,934	14.8
Health & Social Insurance levies	663	7.2	34,570	11.9
Property & related taxes	1,435	15.5	26,456	9.1
Corporate Income tax	1,199	13.0	26,805	9.3
Liquor & tobacco taxes	837	9.1	8,127	2.8
Motive fuel taxes	525	5.7	10,871	3.8
Miscellaneous Taxes	55	0.6	3,837	1.3
Natural Resource Revenues	266	2.9	8,770	3.0
Privileges, Licences & Permits	190	2.1	3,880	1.3
Customs Duties	438	4.7	2,677	0.9
Other Consumption taxes	173	1.9	4,894	1.7
Non-resident taxes	0	0.0	2,138	0.7
Total	9,231		289,748	

Source: Statistics Canada, Public Institutions Division, cats. 68-211, 68-204, 68-207, 68-212, 68-512; calculations by the authors.

1974, all income increases were taxed at progressively higher rates in spite of the fact that much of the increased income represented illusory inflation-based gains. From 1974 to 1985, brackets and exemptions were increased by an "indexing factor" based on the consumer price index. From 1986 onwards, the income-tax system has only been partially indexed because the indexing factor has been set at the amount by which the inflation rate exceeds three percent. Partial indexing means that although the inflation rate was 5.6 percent in 1991, personal income-tax exemptions and brackets increased by only 2.6 percent between 1991 and 1992. Exemptions and brackets are still at their 1992 level because inflation has been below 3.0 percent in every year since 1992. The Organisation for Economic Cooperation and Development (OECD) estimates that between 1988 and 1998, 18 percent of tax filers were pushed into a higher tax bracket because of partial indexation. This translates to 1.4 million Canadians becoming taxable because inflation adjustments were made to their incomes but not to their exemptions. Another 1.9 million taxpayers jumped from the 17 to 26 percent bracket and 0.6 million moved from the 26 to the 29 percent bracket.

As a consequence of this revenue growth, government was able to rely less on other forms of taxation and to allow the burden of some of these taxes to fall. However, in some important cases—notably sales tax and health and social insurance levies—the rate of tax was increased despite rapidly growing revenues from personal income tax. Table 1.2 presents the share of GDP that the top nine taxes represent.

While swelling revenue from income tax poured into the federal government's coffers, the provinces were prompted by their desire for additional tax revenue to boost their sales tax rates. Two general exceptions are Alberta, which has no sales tax, and British Columbia, where the sales tax has been adjusted up and down.

In British Columbia, sales tax was reduced from 7 percent to 5 percent on April 11, 1978 and was further reduced to 4 percent on April 1, 1979. On March 10, 1981, however, it was raised to 6 percent and, in July 1983, raised again to 7 percent. In the 1987 budget, the tax was once again dropped to 6 percent but, in the 1993 budget, raised once more to 7 percent, where it remains.

The federal government also sought to increase its revenue from indirect sources in the early and mid-1980s by increasing its takings from the Manufacturers' Sales Tax and, in 1991, by replacing this tax with the more comprehensive GST. Department of Finance officials hoped to raise an extra $10 billion annually from this new source.

The rise in resource taxation in the 1970s and 1980s resulted primarily from rises in the price of oil and gas, triggered by the oil embargo and subsequent cartelization of oil pricing by the OPEC countries in 1973. In the normal course of events, these price rises in Canada would

Table 1.2: Total Taxes as a Percentage of Gross Domestic Product, 1961 and 1997

	1961	1997
Personal Income taxes	5.1	13.3
General Sales taxes	3.3	5.0
Health & Social Insurance levies	1.6	4.0
Property and related taxes	3.5	3.1
Corporate Income taxes	2.9	3.1
Liquor & Tobacco taxes	2.0	1.0
Import duties	1.1	0.3
Motive Fuel taxes	1.3	1.3
Natural Resource & other taxes	1.7	2.8
Total	22.5	33.9

Source: Statistics Canada, Canadian Economic Observer, cat. 11-010 and Public Institutions Division, cats. 68-211, 68-204, 68-207, 68-212, 68-512; calculations by the authors.

automatically have meant a sharp rise in the return to Canadian producers. But the reaction of provincial governments was to absorb much of this so-called "windfall" or "rent" in the form of higher taxes or royalties. The federal government, for its part, imposed a further tax on producers who were exporting oil. This tax, the oil export charge, amounted to the difference between the controlled Canadian price per barrel and the world price. Proceeds from the federal tax were then used to subsidize imports of foreign oil into the eastern provinces.

From 1974 to 1984, both the provincial and federal governments escalated their energy tax effort but the federal government did so especially. The National Energy Program and the subsequent Energy Agreement allowed the federal government to earn about $4 billion from petroleum during 1984.

The 1985 federal budget incorporated a number of changes to energy taxes as agreed upon in the Western Accord with the governments of Saskatchewan, Alberta, and British Columbia. Both the oil export charge and the petroleum compensation charge were eliminated. Other energy taxes, such as the Petroleum and Gas Revenue Tax, were revised, reduced and, in some cases, phased out. These changes, combined with the decline in world oil prices, has resulted in a decline in energy-related revenues in both relative and absolute terms. (For more information on oil pricing and taxation, see Watkins and Walker 1977).

The late 1980s and early 1990s saw the federal government trying to make income, corporate, and sales taxes more efficient and less of a burden to Canadians competing in the international marketplace. While corporate and income tax *rates* fell, many deductions were eliminated in order to expand the tax *base*. These changes were supposed to lessen the degree to which taxes enter into Canadians' decisions. If this principle seems strange, consider a flat tax. The rate of such a tax is not related to any economic activity in which the individual may engage. Government simply takes a fixed proportion of total income irrespective of how it is earned. What the government takes may be huge but since the tax is not related to how much an individual works or spends, it will not directly affect decisions between, for example, spending and saving or working and not working. In particular, since the taxation rate is the same regardless of income, there is no tax disincentive to make the effort to move to higher income levels from any given starting income.

Lowering tax rates, however, did not lead to less tax collection. In fact, in the past 13 years, federal collections from the average family have risen by $2,450 in 1998 dollars. This rise is due to the expanding tax base and, more recently, to bracket creep. That the federal government has not collected even more taxes is due to its declining commitment to provincial projects such as welfare, education, and health care.

In reaction, the provinces have chosen to make up the shortfall not by reducing spending but by increasing taxes. Since 1985, provincial collections from the average family have increased by $806 in 1998 dollars.

Dividing the spoils

How total tax revenue is divided among different levels of government is one of the important tax questions of the 1990s. Table 1.3 provides a breakdown of major taxes by federal, provincial, and municipal levels of government for the years 1961 and 1997. Total taxes collected now amount to 33.9 cents out of every dollar of GDP, a 51 percent rise since 1961.

These figures do give a somewhat distorted impression because some municipal and provincial government revenue comes from other levels of government. For example, in 1961, fully 30 percent of provincial and municipal revenues were derived from other levels of government. Provinces received transfers from the federal government while municipalities received transfers from both levels.

In the case of provincial revenues, the figures for 1961 reflect the tax agreement that was in effect between the federal and provincial governments. Under the agreement, the federal government rented the provinces' rights to tax personal incomes. In effect, the provinces relinquished their right to tax personal incomes in return for cash payments from the federal government, which collected all the taxes. Accordingly, the tax-collection statistics for 1961 do not reflect the division of the revenues produced but only which level of government actually collected them.

For 1997, the collection figures more closely match the revenue as it was divided between federal and provincial governments because revenue-sharing agreements have been gradually modified to eliminate tax-rental arrangements and shared-cost programs. In the years following 1978, the provinces have had, increasingly, to find their own revenues. As a consequence, tax receipts from different levels of government more closely reflect the actual sharing of tax revenues. To a considerable degree, this evolution reflects the changing attitudes of the partners in Canadian confederation: changing tax arrangements may be the first steps towards a more decentralized federation. For the 1997/98 fiscal year, Alberta expects to receive about 7.0 percent of its revenue from the federal government. This gives Alberta considerably more flexibility when they decide whether or not to participate in new or ongoing federal programs than, for example, Nova Scotia, which receives about 40 percent of its revenue from federal sources.

The relationship between provincial and municipal government revenues reflects a different process. Municipalities now collect much less

Table 1.3: Taxes Collected by Federal, Provincial and Municipal Governments

	Federal ($billions)		Provincial ($billions)		Municipal ($billions)	
	1961	1997	1961	1997	1961	1997
Personal Income taxes	2.0	68.5	0.1	45.3	0.0	0.0
Corporate Income taxes	0.2	16.9	1.0	9.9	0.0	0.0
General Sales taxes	0.3	20.9	1.0	22.0	0.0	0.1
Property tax	0.0	0.0	0.0	7.2	1.3	19.3
Health & Social Insurance levies	0.5	19.8	0.2	14.7	0.0	0.0
Natural Resource revenues	0.0	0.1	0.3	8.7	0.0	0.0
Import duties	0.5	2.7	0.0	0.0	0.0	0.0
Other taxes	0.6	12.1	1.1	21.3	0.1	0.4
Total	4.8	141.0	2.9	129.0	1.4	19.7

Importance of revenue source to level of government (percent)

	Federal		Provincial		Municipal	
	1961	1997	1961	1997	1961	1997
Personal Income taxes	95.2	60.2	4.8	39.8	0.0	0.0
Corporate Income taxes	16.7	62.9	83.3	37.1	0.0	0.0
General Sales taxes	23.1	48.7	76.9	51.1	0.0	0.1
Property tax	0.0	0.0	0.0	27.0	100.0	73.0
Health & Social Insurance levies	71.4	57.4	28.6	42.6	0.0	0.0
Natural Resource revenues	0.0	0.8	100.0	99.2	0.0	0.0
Import duties	100.0	100.0	0.0	0.0	0.0	0.0
Other taxes	33.3	35.9	61.1	63.0	5.6	1.1
Total	52.7	48.7	31.9	44.5	15.4	6.8

Source: Statistics Canada, Public Institutions Division, cats. 68-211, 68-204, 68-207, 68-212, 68-512; calculations by the authors.

of their total revenue in the form of taxes than they did in 1961: fully 29.7 percent of municipal revenue is now accounted for by transfers from federal and provincial governments, mainly the latter. In large part, the emerging role of municipalities as dependencies of the provincial governments is a result of decreasing reliance on property taxation as a form of finance (see table 1.1 and figure 1.3). Property taxes accounted for only 9.1 percent of total taxes in 1997, down from 15.5 percent in 1961.

Figure 1.3: Where Government Obtained Its Revenue in 1961 and 1997

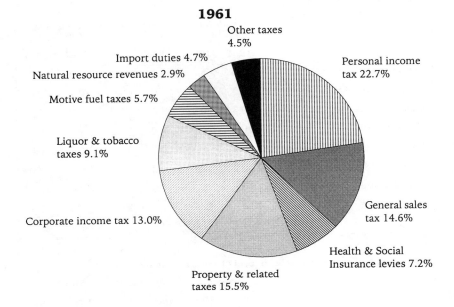

1961

Other taxes 4.5%

Import duties 4.7%

Natural resource revenues 2.9%

Motive fuel taxes 5.7%

Liquor & tobacco taxes 9.1%

Corporate income tax 13.0%

Property & related taxes 15.5%

Personal income tax 22.7%

General sales tax 14.6%

Health & Social Insurance levies 7.2%

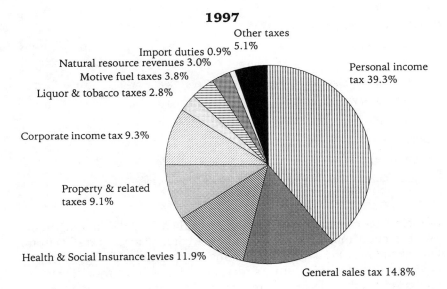

1997

Other taxes 5.1%

Import duties 0.9%

Natural resource revenues 3.0%

Motive fuel taxes 3.8%

Liquor & tobacco taxes 2.8%

Corporate income tax 9.3%

Property & related taxes 9.1%

Health & Social Insurance levies 11.9%

Personal income tax 39.3%

General sales tax 14.8%

Source: Table 1.1. Note that percentages may not add due to rounding.

The fifth column—hidden taxation

Most people are aware that they pay income tax, sales tax, and property tax—the so-called direct taxes. Many others correctly regard contributions by employees and employers to the Employment Insurance fund and the Canada and Quebec Pension Plans as taxes. Similarly, many families know how much of these taxes they pay, either in terms of the rate (*e.g.* provincial sales taxes), or the total amount (*e.g.* property and income taxes). There are, however, many taxes of which Canadians, by and large, are unaware. These taxes are built into the price of goods and services and are not identified to the final consumer as a tax. For want of a better name, we call these "implicit" or "hidden" taxes.

Indirect taxes

There are several different kinds of hidden tax. The most well known of these are the so-called indirect taxes—principally excise taxes on such items as tobacco and alcohol, value-added taxes (GST), and import duties. These taxes are paid by some intermediary in the production process and become incorporated in the final price of the product. The most notorious examples are tobacco, liquor, and gasoline taxes. See figures 1.4 and 1.5, respectively, for a breakdown of taxes paid for a litre of gasoline and a bottle of liquor and table 1.4 for the break-down

Table 1.4: Components of the Price of Gasoline (in cents per litre for regular unleaded gasoline at self-serve pumps), by City

	Crude cost (estimate)	Federal tax	Provincial tax	Refining and marketing costs, and profit	Retail margin	Total price
Vancouver	18.0	14.0	15.0	11.8	2.8	61.6
Calgary	17.1	13.4	9.0	9.2	3.9	52.6
Regina	17.4	14.0	15.0	11.3	2.9	60.6
Winnipeg	17.6	13.8	11.5	10.7	4.3	57.9
Toronto	18.3	13.5	14.7	5.5	1.9	53.9
Montreal	17.0	13.8	20.4	6.1	3.7	61.0
Saint John	16.5	13.8	15.1	12.3	5.1	62.8
Halifax	16.5	13.7	17.8	7.9	5.4	61.3
Charlottetown	16.5	14.2	12.0	15.7	5.5	63.9
St. John's	16.3	14.2	21.3	11.6	6.0	69.4
Canadian Av.	17.6	13.7	15.2	7.8	3.1	57.4

Source: Petroleum Communication Foundation.

Figure 1.4: Government Take from a Litre of Gasoline (Canadian average; in cents per litre)

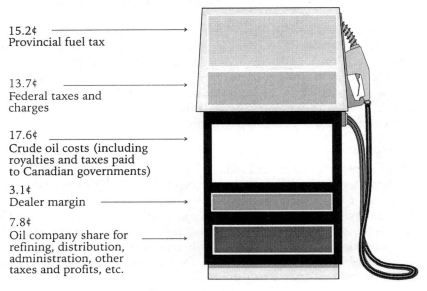

15.2¢
Provincial fuel tax

13.7¢
Federal taxes and charges

17.6¢
Crude oil costs (including royalties and taxes paid to Canadian governments)

3.1¢
Dealer margin

7.8¢
Oil company share for refining, distribution, administration, other taxes and profits, etc.

Average price per litre: 57.4¢

Source: Table 1.4.

by province of the pump price of gasoline. In the case of liquor, the federal rate of indirect tax is 132 percent. In addition, alcohol bears the provincial government's mark-up as well as a provincial sales tax. The final delivered price of alcohol is 577 percent above the price received by the distiller. The taxes on tobacco were so high that they led to widespread smuggling and tax evasion until 1994 when taxes were sharply reduced east of the Manitoba border; the western provinces stepped up enforcement instead of cutting taxes. According to an article in the *Globe and Mail*, smuggling had become so bad that, as Ontario's finance minister at the time put it, "It reached a point where the retail market in cigarettes in Ontario was in complete shambles." (McInnes 1996: A1, A4). Most consumers of these products are aware that alcohol and tobacco are highly taxed but rarely do they know the actual rate of tax and the amount of tax that they are paying.

During 1997, total indirect taxes of all kinds amounted to $96 billion in Canada. This was 11.2 percent of total Canadian income and accounted for 33.1 percent of total government revenue from taxation. In other words, quite apart from the tax they pay when they receive their

Figure 1.5: Typical Government Take from a Bottle of Liquor

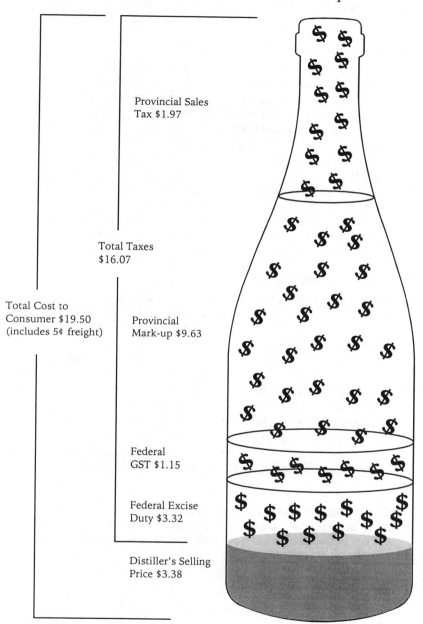

Provincial Sales
Tax $1.97

Total Taxes
$16.07

Total Cost to
Consumer $19.50
(includes 5¢ freight)

Provincial
Mark-up $9.63

Federal
GST $1.15

Federal Excise
Duty $3.32

Distiller's Selling
Price $3.38

Source: Association of Canadian Distillers, 1997.

incomes, Canadians pay, on average, a further 11.2 percent in indirect taxes when they spend their income. Furthermore, almost one-third of all government revenue is collected in this indirect, hidden form.

The hot potatoes—passing tax forward

Hidden taxes are hard to calculate because people try to pass them on to others—any tax that can be avoided is money in one's own pocket. As a result, people throughout the economy are constantly attempting to avoid situations in which they will have to pay taxes, and seeking to pay as little tax as possible when they cannot avoid them. The moonlighting tradesperson who engages in "cash only" transactions, the mechanic who fixes his neighbour's truck in return for free cartage, the dentist who fixes the teeth of a fellow dentist's family on a reciprocal basis, the tycoon whose business is incorporated in the Turks and Caicos Islands, all want to avoid taxes. In the end, though, when a tax is levied, somebody ends up paying. One of the most difficult and important questions in economics is to discover who that somebody is; this is known as the study of "tax incidence."

How employees pass the tax on

To get an idea of the difficulties involved, consider the following. The average Canadian employee measures his welfare in terms of after-tax dollars and in each new wage bargain aims to get an increase in take-home pay. The fact that an increase in gross terms will imply a smaller increase in after-tax dollars motivates the employee or his union representative to demand a larger gross increase. By doing so, the employee is attempting to get the employer to bear the burden of the additional tax. For an example of this process, see table 1.5.

Expressed slightly differently, the employee who bargains in this manner is attempting to pass the tax forward. This behavior is not unique; it is a general characteristic of all participants in the Canadian economy. Corporations attempt to pass the higher taxes on profits and

---

Table 1.5: Take-Home Pay versus Gross Pay

In 1997, a single person in Ontario with an income of $35,000 had to receive a 6.5% raise in pay to realize a 5% increase in after-tax pay. Comparable figures for the other provinces are presented below.

NF	PE	NS	NB	QC	ON	MB	SK	AB	BC
6.8%	6.6%	6.6%	6.7%	6.8%	6.5%	6.8%	6.7%	6.4%	6.5%

Source: Canadian Tax Foundation, Finances of the Nation, 1997; calculations by the authors.

payroll forward to the consumer in the form of higher prices or backward to employees in the form of lower wages. The difficulty in measuring the degree to which these attempts are or are not successful greatly complicates the study of tax incidence.

Who pays the indirect taxes?

While it is difficult to know where the burden of these taxes ultimately lies, it is not impossible. We need to make intelligent assumptions about how each tax is passed on. For example, a general sales tax is collected and remitted to government by retailers. It is clear, however, that in most cases the retailers do not actually bear the tax—they are merely the agents for collecting it. The actual effect of the tax is to increase the price of all goods and services affected by the tax, and to cause a corresponding reduction in the purchasing power of family incomes. Accordingly, to the extent that a general sales tax causes an increase in the general level of prices, the tax is borne not by the collectors but by income earners in the economy, whose incomes now buy less. Indirect or sales taxes, therefore, burden all income earned in the economy.

Payroll taxes such as Employment Insurance premiums and contributions to the Canada and Quebec Pension Plans are collected, in part, from the employer and, in part, from the employee. And, while no one would dispute that the employee pays the employee's portion, in most cases it is true that the employee also pays the so-called employer's portion. This is because the payroll tax paid by the employer is included in the total amount of money the employer has available to pay labour-related costs. In other words, payroll taxes reduce potential wage and salary payments below what they would otherwise have been. Since no corresponding reduction can be expected in the price of the products that the employee will want to purchase, the payroll tax, in effect, burdens the employee.

While both of these arguments have been framed in terms of employees and their wages and salaries, it is clear that taxes burden capital income as well. For example, a general sales tax reduces the purchasing power of all income, not just wage and salary income. As a result, it is appropriate to view the burden of the general sales tax as falling on all forms of income, including interest income and dividends. All of the estimates of tax burden constructed in this study, therefore, allocate the burden of general sales taxes in proportion to all income received by a family. In practical terms, this means that if general sales taxes amount to 6 percent of total Canadian income in a particular year, we add 6 percent of a family's total income to the family's tax bill when we calculate how much tax the family pays.

In computing this burden of general sales tax, income that a family receives from government is explicitly ignored. This is because the payments received from government, such as Old Age Security and the Canada Pension Plan, have been and are currently either directly or indirectly indexed to the general level of prices to offset the effects of inflation. As the general price level rises in step with the sales tax, the purchasing power of transfers from government is not permitted to fall. As a consequence, the general sales tax does not have the effect of burdening income in this form, and it would be inappropriate to allocate any part of the burden of general sales taxes to this sort of income.

While the burdens of a general sales tax and payroll taxes are relatively straightforward to assign, the assignment of particular excise taxes is more elusive. Whereas a general sales tax increases all prices and hence reduces the purchasing power of all incomes not derived from transfers from government, particular taxes on commodities usually affect only the price of that commodity. For example, excise taxes imposed on liquor, motor vehicles, and fuels affect only the prices of those products. Ultimately, of course, they may affect a whole range of prices—fuel taxes and motor vehicle taxes affect the price of transportation. These taxes may, therefore, have an overall effect although levied only on a particular product.

In light of these considerations, it has been the usual practice when calculating tax burdens to allocate the burden of particular excise taxes according to the consumption of those items. Studies of the 1976 tax burden published by The Fraser Institute (Walker 1976; Pipes and Walker 1979) employed this methodology. Following this methodology, however, gives rise to a variety of problems. First, only the first-round effects of the excise tax are incorporated and, hence, the actual distribution of the tax burden may differ substantially from the estimate. Second, this method may not even provide good estimates of the first-round effects of the tax because the relative burden of a particular tax borne by a family is determined not by the family's consumption of the taxed item but by the fraction of the family's income spent on the item relative to the national average.

In view of these problems with the traditional approach, and given that the proportions of income spent on different items by various income groups do not vary widely from the average, we decided, for the purposes of this study, to distribute excise taxes in the same way as general sales taxes; that is to say, this study assumes that excise taxes burden total incomes—excluding government transfers to persons.

So, the answer to the question, "Who pays the indirect taxes?" is ultimately a straightforward one. Although indirect taxes appear in a variety of forms, they burden the income that the family earns.

Other taxes by other names

In addition to "formal" taxes levied by government, there are a variety of other government actions that have the same effect as taxes but are not normally identified as such. These activities are becoming an increasingly prominent feature of the Canadian economic landscape and require special mention.

Clothing and textile taxes

In November 1976, the federal government imposed a quota on imported clothing and textiles. Its purpose was to limit the importation of inexpensive clothing and textiles and so protect Canadian clothing and textile manufacturers from competition. The associated decline in competition for the Canadian consumer's clothing-expenditure dollar undoubtedly produced a higher price for clothing than would otherwise have existed.

The difference between the price for clothing that would have prevailed in the absence of the quota and the price that actually prevails is a tax on the consumer. Proceeds from this tax go directly to producers and are, in effect, a subsidy of the producers. There is no difference in principle between this sort of tax and the other hidden taxes that we presented above. Of course, these "clothing taxes" do not show up in government revenue figures and precise estimates of their size are difficult to make, but we cannot ignore their existence.

Some of the burden associated with tariffs and quotas has been eliminated as a result of the North American Free Trade Agreement between Canada, the United States, and Mexico. However, in many cases the principal source of cheaper products is not the United States but less developed countries. In value terms, 77.4 percent of textile imports into Canada come from developed countries while 71.5 percent of clothing imports came from developing countries (Canadian Textiles Institute, personal communication to Joel Emes, 1998).

The authors of *Free Trade between the United States and Canada* estimated that the total amount of tax levied in the form of tariff protection or other barriers to international competition may be as high as 10.5 percent of Canada's Gross National Product (Wonnacott and Wonnacott 1967: 299).

Marketing-board taxes

There are dozens of cartels controlling farm products in Canada. These cartels or marketing boards generally have the effect of suppressing competition in the production of the product subject to the cartel, and they consequently cause the price of the product to be higher than it would otherwise have been. As in the case of imports of clothing and textiles restricted by tariffs, the amount by which the marketing board price exceeds the price that would prevail in its absence—that is, in the open market—is a tax on the consumer. Accordingly, marketing boards ought to be viewed as a device for transferring money from consumers to producers. This transfer is thus equivalent to a tax on consumers, the proceeds of which are given to producers.

The OECD estimates that Canada's Consumer Subsidy Equivalent (CSE) for 1997 was $2.2 billion. The CSE measures the implicit taxes imposed on consumers by agricultural policy. Using the OECD's assumption that food expenditures represent about 10 percent of personal expenditures, marketing boards and other implicit agricultural taxes add about 4.3 percent to the cost of the average family's food bill.

According to the OECD, the overall level of support to the agricultural sector has been falling since 1986 and recently there has been a shift away from supporting the market price towards making direct payments to producers. The dairy sector, Canada's most heavily supported agricultural sector, remains unreformed. Dairy accounts for more than 50 percent of Canada's total support and 90 percent of all market price support.

The meeting of OECD agricultural ministers in March 1998 focussed on two main themes: an evaluation of policy over the last ten years and the need for continued reform of the agricultural sector. The level of agricultural support in OECD countries has seen a slow, steady decline since 1986 due to increased trade liberalization. If this process continues, and especially if the Canadian dairy sector is reformed, Canadian consumers will face lower implicit taxes.

A study by Moroz and Brown (1987) tried to measure the costs of some of the hidden taxes mentioned above. They estimated the dollar value of protection to Canadian industries in 1979 due to tariffs and non-tariff barriers such as import quotas. The sum of such protection across industries was $35.1 billion in 1997 dollars. Most of the protection went to textiles, agriculture, and forestry. In sum, each Canadian paid $1,159 (in 1997 dollars) in hidden taxes on internationally traded items in 1979.

Regulatory taxation

In general, a government can achieve a given objective either by taxation and subsidization or by regulation; rather than imposing import quotas, the federal government could have assisted Canadian clothing manufacturers by giving them a direct subsidy financed from general tax revenue. That the government chooses to use regulation to convey a subsidy in this fashion should not distract attention from the fact that a subsidy is being provided and that it is the Canadian consumer who is paying for it.

For governments, regulation seems to be a painless way of advancing their public policy without spending tax dollars directly. The reality of regulation is not so benign since it increases the cost of doing business. According to a recent Fraser Institute study, the cost of all federal, provincial, and municipal regulations amounted to $83.4 billion in 1995/96 (Mihlar 1998). This works out to $11,272 dollars per family of four. The federal and provincial governments have legislated over 100,000 regulations over the last 22 years; the federal government alone passed an average of 1,031 regulations per year.

Deferred taxation

During his budget statement in November 1978, the Honourable Jean Chrétien, then Federal Minister of Finance, made much of the fact that, because the personal income tax structure had been indexed to inflation, there had, in effect, been a reduction in personal income taxation compared to what would have prevailed in the absence of indexing. That is to say, exemptions had been increased by the rate of inflation and tax brackets had been shifted to ensure that incomes swollen by inflation would not be taxed more heavily on that account alone. While this change in the tax structure, discussed in more detail above, was indeed a welcome one, it did not represent a move towards a permanent reduction in the government's propensity to tax.

In fact, the "reduction" in personal income tax revenues was accompanied—starting in 1975—by deficits in the federal government's accounts that were unprecedented in peacetime. Although this situation is not entirely attributable to the decline in personal income-tax revenues, it is clear that continued growth in income taxation would have meant a smaller deficit and a reduction in net cash requirements to be financed by issuing debt. Accordingly, it has been standard practice in assessing Canada's current level of taxation to take into account the extent to which tax collections are merely deferred by current tax "reductions."

In other words, when calculating the total tax burden of all government operations in a given year, we usually include not only taxes levied but also future taxes that must be levied to discharge debts acquired by the government to finance the current deficit. In recent years, there has been a dramatic shift away from deficit financing, or deferred taxation, in favour of balanced or surplus budgets. This shift has made the calculation of a balanced budget tax burden largely unnecessary.

How much tax should Canadians pay?

In 1917, when he first introduced the Personal Income Tax, the Finance Minister, Sir Thomas White, was of the opinion that no Canadian should pay tax on income less than $2,000 if he were single and had no dependents. Married taxpayers, he said, should pay tax on income in excess of $3,000. The tax structure that ultimately evolved provided that single Canadians paid income tax on income in excess of $1,500, while married Canadians were exempted from the tax until their incomes exceeded $3,000. However, in the very next year, this was reduced to $2,000 for a married taxpayer and $1,000 for single Canadians (Government of Canada 1917).

While the tax structure has gone through many changes in the intervening years, it is interesting to ask how Canadians would be taxed if this initial view of the "ability to pay" had kept pace with developments in people's incomes. To answer this question we have adjusted the original exemption levels by the increase in inflation over the period since 1917. This adjustment yields an exemption level for 1997 of $11,447 for single taxpayers and $22,894 for married taxpayers. But actual personal credits for single and married taxpayers amounted to $6,456 and $11,836 in 1997—significantly less than the level of income that would have been exempt if the 1917 standard had continued in force.

The reason for the disparity is that, over the years from 1917 to 1974, exemption levels were not indexed to the cost of living or the increase in family incomes—in fact, in a few years during the Depression, exemption levels were actually reduced. As we saw above, exemption levels have been fully or partially indexed to the rate of inflation since 1974.

Chapter 2
Personal Income Taxation in Canada

PERSONAL INCOME TAX is the largest single source of government revenue. It follows, therefore, that the largest single tax paid by the average Canadian family is the income tax. This tax came into existence in 1917 as a "temporary" emergency measure to help finance the increasing debt incurred during World War I. Nothing, it seems, endures like the temporary.

The current income tax structure

The federal and provincial governments share personal income taxation. Except for Quebec, which operates its own system, the provinces base their personal income tax on the "basic federal rate." When your personal income tax bill is calculated, the first portion goes to the federal government based on which "basic federal rate" applies to you (17 percent, 26 percent, or 29 percent). The next portion goes to the provincial government. This is calculated as a percent of the portion already allocated for the federal government, which is why one often hears the provincial tax system referred to as a "tax on a tax." After your basic federal and provincial portions are calculated, the final step in determining your personal tax bill is to add any high-income surtaxes that may apply.

Table 2.1 presents the actual income-tax rates (combined federal and provincial) encountered by the average single individual at various taxable income levels in 1992 and 1997. As the figures show, the minimum rate of tax is 26.35 percent, payable on the range of taxable

Table 2.1: Marginal Rates (rate of tax in percent on the next dollar of income), 1992 and 1997, for Combined Federal and Provincial Personal Income Tax

Taxable Income 1992		Taxable Income 1997	
$1–$29,590	26.61%	$1–$29,590	26.35%
$29,591–$59,180	40.69%	$29,591–$59,180	40.30%
$59,181 and above	46.84%	$59,181–$63,437	44.95%
		$63,438 and above	46.40%

Sources: Canadian Tax Foundation, The National Finances 1993, 1993; Finances of The Nation 1997, 1997.

income from $1.00 to $29,590. The second rate is 40.30 percent, payable on the range of taxable income from $29,591 to $59,180. The third rate is 44.95 percent, payable on the range of taxable income from $59,181 to $63,437. The maximum rate of 46.40 percent is payable on taxable income in excess of $63,437. These rates are the marginal rates of tax encountered as one moves from one level of taxable income to the next. Table 2.2 shows the combined federal and provincial marginal tax rates for a single individual in each province at three levels of income. An equally interesting series of calculations relates to the amount of tax an individual pays on a given amount of total income (not taxable income). These rates are shown in table 2.3.

Table 2.2: Personal Income Tax for a Single Taxpayer, Combined Federal and Provincial Marginal Rates (in percent), 1997

	Income		
	$20,000	$50,000	$100,000
Newfoundland	29.2	44.7	53.3
Prince Edward Island	27.6	43.8	50.3
Nova Scotia	27.5	42.0	50.0
New Brunswick	28.2	43.2	51.1
Quebec	36.1	47.1	52.9
Ontario	25.7	39.3	51.6
Manitoba	30.3	44.3	50.4
Saskatchewan	29.1	45.5	51.9
Alberta	25.7	40.1	46.1
British Columbia	26.2	40.0	54.2

Source: Finances of The Nation, 1997, Canadian Tax Foundation, 1997.

Table 2.3: Combined Federal and Provincial Personal Income Tax and Tax Rate (Single Taxpayer with No Dependants), 1997

Total Income ($)	Total Tax Payable ($)	Rate (%)
7,500	(33)	(0.4)
10,000	537	5.4
12,500	1,124	9.0
15,000	1,744	11.6
17,500	2,364	13.5
20,000	2,985	14.9
25,000	4,226	16.9
30,000	5,727	19.1
50,000	13,774	27.5
100,000	36,353	36.4
200,000	82,753	41.4

Sources: Canadian Tax Foundation, Finances of The Nation 1997, 1997; calculations by the authors.

In the case of families, the situation can be slightly different because there are credits permitted for the dependent spouse. Support of children also eases somewhat the tax burden on the taxpayer. In perusing tax rates for the average family of four presented in table 2.4, the reader should bear in mind that this schedule of rates is not applicable

Table 2.4: Combined Federal & Provincial Personal Income Tax and Tax Rate (Married Taxpayer with Two Dependent Children under 16 Years of Age), 1997

Total Income ($)	Total Tax Payable ($)	Rate (%)
17,500	(2,110)	-12.1
20,000	(1,490)	-7.5
25,000	159	0.6
30,000	1,957	6.5
50,000	11,307	22.6
100,000	34,889	34.9
200,000	81,289	40.6

Sources: Canadian Tax Foundation, Finances of The Nation 1997, 1997; calculations by the authors.

to all families. In many cases, both adult members of the family declare taxable income. In this case, they each file a separate return, and tax rates for individuals apply. Of course, this is to the advantage of the tax-payers. If, for example, a childless couple who are both working have the same income—say $25,000 per year—they pay total tax of about $8,452 when they file as individuals. If their total income of $50,000 were earned by only one of them, their total tax payable would be about $12,356—a difference of $3,904.

In other words, if their income is earned by one family member, the family pays a gross tax rate of 24.7 percent but if their income is composed of two salaries, the tax rate is only 16.9 percent. The difference between the two tax rates rises as family income increases until very high income levels are reached (see table 2.5). This difference between the tax rates of families with a single income and those with double incomes affects many of the other calculations in the remainder of this book. In particular, income tax payments shown in the various composite tax tables in chapter 3 reflect the fact that, on average, tax payments are made by a mixture of single-taxpayer and double-taxpayer families.

Who pays the income tax bill?

According to data for 1996 from Revenue Canada, a total of $96.5 billion in income taxes was paid by individuals and, as table 2.6 shows, 43 percent of it was paid by individuals with incomes below $50,000. Individuals with incomes below $60,000 paid 56 percent of the total income tax bill. In fact, 39 percent of all income taxes were paid by individuals with yearly incomes in the relatively narrow range of $20,000 to $50,000.

Table 2.5: Tax Rates For a Married Couple, 1997

Total family income ($)	One income earner		Two income earners	
	Tax ($)	Tax Rate (%)	Tax ($)	Tax Rate (%)
15,000	326	2.2	(66)	−0.4
20,000	1,567	7.8	1,074	5.4
25,000	2,808	11.2	2,248	9.0
30,000	4,309	14.4	3,488	11.6
50,000	12,356	24.7	8,452	16.9
100,000	34,889	34.9	27,548	27.5
200,000	81,289	40.6	72,706	36.4

Sources: Canadian Tax Foundation, Finances of The Nation 1997, 1997; calculations by the authors.

Table 2.6: Income, Taxes, and Tax Returns by Income Group, 1996

Total income assessed ($000s)	Percentage of total tax paid by this income group	Percentage of total tax paid by all groups at or below this income group	Percentage of total returns filed by this income group	Percentage of total returns filed by all groups at or below this income group	Percentage of total income declared by this income group	Percentage of total income declared by all groups at or below this income group
loss or nil	0.00	0.00	3.50	3.50	-0.16	-0.16
.001-10	0.24	0.25	23.45	26.95	4.70	4.54
10-15	1.54	1.79	15.16	42.11	7.05	11.59
15-20	3.18	4.97	10.00	52.11	6.54	18.13
20-25	4.61	9.58	8.31	60.41	7.02	25.14
25-30	5.97	15.55	7.63	68.05	7.89	33.03
30-35	6.75	22.29	6.51	74.55	7.93	40.97
35-40	7.24	29.53	5.40	79.95	7.60	48.57
40-45	7.14	36.67	4.29	84.24	6.85	55.42
45-50	6.80	43.47	3.40	87.65	6.07	61.49
50-60	12.17	55.65	4.93	92.58	10.14	71.63
60-70	8.98	64.63	2.87	95.45	6.96	78.59
70-80	5.73	70.36	1.50	96.95	4.21	82.80
80-90	3.85	74.22	0.85	97.80	2.71	85.51
90-100	2.71	76.93	0.52	98.32	1.84	87.35
100-150	6.90	83.83	0.98	99.30	4.40	91.74
150-250	5.56	89.39	0.44	99.75	3.14	94.88
250,000+	10.61	100.00	0.25	100.00	5.12	100.00

Sources: Revenue Canada, Tax Statistics on Individuals, 1996 Tax Year, (Interim Statistics—Universe Data), 1998; calculations by the authors.

As column 4 of table 2.6 shows, over one-half of all taxable returns were filed by individuals with incomes less than $20,000. This proportion reflects the large number of part-time workers, students employed during the summer, and other intermittent workers earning low incomes. These taxpayers generated only 5.0 percent of total tax revenue, while the top 25.5 percent of taxpayers—those declaring income of $35,000 or more—contributed 77.7 percent of the total income tax bill.

An interesting aspect of the information in table 2.6 is the relation between taxes paid and income declared. For example, while 22.3 percent of the total income tax bill was paid by individuals with incomes below $35,000, column 6 reveals that this group earned 41.0 percent of all the income declared. So, income earners below $35,000 paid a smaller proportion of the total tax bill than their share of total earned income might suggest. On the other hand, the top 22.3 percent of taxpayers, those who had incomes in excess of $35,000, paid about 77.7 percent of the total tax bill, while receiving only 59.0 percent of total income earned.

The reason for this, of course, is the fact that the income tax structure is "progressive." That is, it takes a larger fraction from high incomes than it does from low incomes, as is clear from the tax rates presented in table 2.4. Sales taxes also contribute to progressivity even though everyone pays the same rate irrespective of income, because sales tax rebates vary inversely with income. Furthermore, many income transfers from the state are indexed to the price of goods, so that as the price rises due to a sales tax, so do the transfers. This eases the burden of sales taxes to the poor.

Chapter 3
How Much Tax
Do You
Really Pay?

WHILE INCOME TAX is the single largest tax category, it represents less than half of the total taxes paid by the average Canadian family. The purpose of this chapter is to expand the discussion to include all taxes that Canadians pay.

How much income do you really earn?

Cash income

In order to calculate properly how much tax a person or group pays, it is necessary first to determine their income. This is a complex calculation because there are a multitude of sources of income other than wages and salaries. This chapter explains the method for deriving the income figures used in subsequent sections.

The ultimate goal of income calculations is to determine the total income a Canadian citizen would have if there were no taxes of any sort and other factors remained unchanged. To arrive at such a figure, it is necessary to determine all the income sources a person might have, and all of the taxes that would have been paid on this income before the person received it.

The first layer of income items is easily discovered: wages, salaries, interest from savings bonds, or rent from the in-law suite in the basement are the sorts of items that make up cash income.

Cash income and under-reporting

In its regular surveys of household income, Statistics Canada finds that people typically omit some income items when they estimate their cash income. That is, they under-report their income. The particular items omitted vary from family to family, but, on average, families tend to underestimate their total income by 4 to 12 percent. Items that might be omitted include miscellaneous interest income, income from "moonlighting," and so on. Fortunately, Statistics Canada does have a comprehensive measure of income in the National Accounts framework, and it is therefore possible not only to know that the survey information is incorrect but also to adjust that information to make it more accurate. Accordingly, estimates of cash income used in this study have been adjusted to make them consistent with the comprehensive income figures contained in the National Accounts.

It may be useful at this stage to provide an example based on a fictitious individual. In order to make the example as comprehensive as possible, it is assumed that the individual has income from all of the sources identified in the study—an unlikely circumstance for any real person. The example is presented in table 3.1.

Total income

In addition to cash income, most families also have various forms of non-cash income that must be included in a comprehensive income figure. For example, most wage and salary earners receive fringe benefits as a condition of their employment and their income also includes the investment income accumulated by their pension plan and the interest accumulated—though not paid—on their insurance policies.

Table 3.1: Cash Income, 1998

Wages & salaries	$35,994
Income from farm operations	183
Unincorporated non-farm income	1,811
Interest	1,451
Dividends	562
Private pension payments	1,458
Government pension payments	498
Old age pension payments	1,370
Other transfers from government	6,669
Total cash income	$49,996

Source: The Fraser Institute, 1998.

At a higher level of subtlety, a comprehensive income total should also include a number of other income sources. For example, income must be imputed on account of interest-free loans that people make. The interest foregone is, in fact, implicit income in the form of a gift.

Profits not paid out as dividends by corporations but held in the form of retained earnings are income of the shareholders of the corporation, even though they do not receive it in the year in which it is reported. Finally, food consumed by farm operators is evaluated at market price and attributed to farm operators as income.

Again, to make the calculation clear, the total income figure is accumulated in table 3.2 for a fictitious individual who is assumed to have income from all sources.

Total income before tax

Some of the income earned by Canadians is taxed before they receive it. For example, shareholders receive dividends on corporate profits after corporate profit taxes have been paid. In the absence of taxes, the dividends or retained earnings of the shareholder would have been higher. Therefore, in order to arrive at total income before tax, it is necessary to add back the tax on corporate profits collected from corporations. Similarly, if there were no property taxes, net after-tax rental income would be higher than it actually is. Therefore, before-tax income must be augmented by the amount of property taxes paid.

Indirect and hidden taxes reduce the effective income available to Canadians because they increase the prices of items that people buy with their incomes. In effect, income after tax is less, in terms of what it will buy, than it was before the tax. In order to arrive at an estimate of before-tax income it is necessary, therefore, to add back to incomes the reduction brought about by indirect taxes. Payroll taxes levied on firms are, as noted earlier, effectively paid by employees, because the

Table 3.2: Total Income, 1998

Cash income (from table 3.1)	$49,996
Fringe benefits from employment	5,279
Investment income from insurance companies	1,002
Investment income from trusteed pension plans	1,318
Imputed interest	315
Value of food from farms	17
Corporate retained earnings	1,053
Total income	$58,981
Source: The Fraser Institute, 1998.	

taxes reduce the amount of money available to pay wages and salaries. Accordingly, it is necessary to add back the amount of payroll taxes to employees' incomes to arrive at a before-tax total income estimate.

Table 3.3 presents an example of a complete income calculation for a fictitious individual who is assumed to have income from all of the income sources identified in the study and to have paid all of the identified taxes.

Calculating the total tax bill

Basically, the tax calculation for the average Canadian family consists of adding up the various taxes that the family pays. Hidden taxes such as taxes on tobacco and alcohol are allocated according to the method

Table 3.3: Total Income before Tax, 1998

Wages & salaries	$35,994
Income from farm operations	183
Unincorporated non-farm income	1,811
Interest	1,451
Dividends	562
Private pension payments	1,458
Government pension payments	498
Old age pension payments	1,370
Other transfers from government	6,669
Total cash income	$49,996
Plus	
Fringe benefits from employment	5,279
Investment income from insurance companies	1,002
Investment income from trusteed pension plans	1,318
Imputed interest	315
Value of food from farms	17
Corporate retained earnings	1,053
Total income	$58,981
Plus	
Property taxes	1,884
Profit taxes	1,958
Indirect taxes	9,871
Total income before tax	$72,695

Source: The Fraser Institute, 1998.

described in chapter 1. To preserve consistency, the family used for the example of the tax calculation in table 3.4 is the same family used in the income calculation.

Table 3.4: Tax Bill of the Average Canadian Family, 1998

Cash income (from table 3.1)	$49,996
Total income before tax (from table 3.3)	72,695
Taxes	
Income taxes	8,466
Sales taxes	3,742
Liquor, tobacco, amusement & other excise taxes	1,526
Automobile, fuel, & motor vehicle licence taxes	728
Social security, medical & hospital taxes	4,024
Property taxes	1,884
Import duties	205
Profits tax	1,958
Natural resource taxes	217
Other taxes	467
Total taxes	$23,218
Taxes as a percentage of cash income	46%
Taxes as a percentage of total income before tax	32%

Source: The Fraser Institute, 1998.

Chapter 4
The Canadian Consumer Tax Index and Tax Freedom Day

IT IS ALWAYS SATISFYING to find one number, or index, that neatly summarizes a complicated issue. It is seldom the case that such a number exists. IQ scores, for instance, do not say everything about an individual's intelligence, and the speed of a computer chip can only give a rough idea of how that computer will perform. The same is true of Canadian taxes. Our system is complex and there is no single number that can give us a complete idea of who pays how much, and how the system has changed over time. That said, we can introduce two of the better indicators of the state of the Canadian tax system: the Canadian Consumer Tax Index and Tax Freedom Day.

The Canadian Consumer Tax Index

For individual taxpayers, the most interesting variable is how much tax they actually have to pay. In The Fraser Institute's first tax study, *How Much Tax Do You Really Pay?* (Walker 1976b), we devised an index that we called the Canadian Consumer Tax Index (CCTI). Its purpose was to provide a summary-at-a-glance of what has been happening to the tax bill faced by the average Canadian family over the years since 1961.

Some readers of that book found the tax index too simple—it failed to take into account how the tax money was spent by governments and, therefore, showed only one side of the ledger (McGillivray 1976). On the other hand, the index in that first study and in all subsequent studies has been widely used by financial and consumer affairs columnists across the country to describe how the Canadian tax system

Table 4.1: The Canadian Consumer Tax Index (1961=100)

Year	Index	Year	Index
1961	100	1990	1,219
1969	186	1992	1,216
1974	324	1994	1,267
1976	357	1996	1,354
1981	682	1998	1,386
1985	886		

Source: The Fraser Institute, 1998.

has evolved. Moreover, it has been in continuous use ever since its release and has been described as the most up-to-date measure of the extent of Canadian taxation.

During 1988, Statistics Canada approached The Fraser Institute to enquire how the CCTI is calculated. That interest was motivated by the advent in Canada of the broadly applied Goods and Services Tax and the desire on the part of the agency to provide a measure of the impact that the new tax would have on the rate of inflation. In 1990, Statistics Canada indicated that it would not proceed because of the methodological problems that would be associated with such a measurement. In view of the high political interest that would attach to such a number, one can appreciate their reluctance.

What is the Canadian Consumer Tax Index?

The Canadian Consumer Tax Index tracks the total tax bill paid by a Canadian family with average income. The "consumer" in question is the taxpaying family, which can be thought of as consuming government services. The Consumer Price Index measures the average price that consumers pay for the goods and services that they buy of their own choice. The CCTI measures the price of goods and services that government buys on behalf of its constituents (see table 4.1 and figure 4.1).

The CCTI is constructed by calculating the difference in the tax bill of an average Canadian family from the tax bill in the base year of 1961 for each of the years included in the index. Now, while each of these families had average income in the year selected, the family is not the same one from year to year. The objective is not to trace the tax experience of a particular family but rather to plot the experience of a family that was average in each year.

The CCTI thus answers the following question: How has the tax burden of the average family changed since 1961, bearing in mind that the average family has itself changed in that period? We can note, for example, that the average family in 1998 is headed by a younger per-

Figure 4.1: The Canadian Consumer Tax Index, 1961–1998

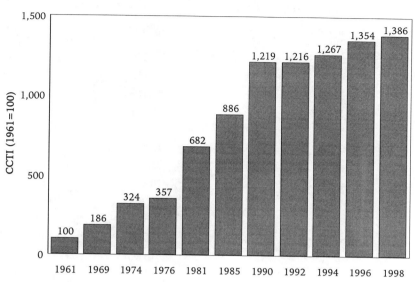

Source: Table 4.1.

son, one who is more likely to own a car but less likely to own a house, and has fewer members than the average family in 1961. Most important, the family's earned income increased by 900 percent over the period.

The basis of the CCTI is the total tax calculation presented in the "Tax Bill" column of table 4.2. Calculations of income and tax were made for a selection of years beginning in 1961 and ending in 1998. The results show that the tax bill of the average Canadian family has increased by 1,286 percent from 1961 and that the index has a value of 1,386 for 1998.

At least part of that increase reflects the effects of inflation. In order to eliminate the effect of the declining value of the dollar, we have also calculated the tax index in real dollars—that is, dollars of 1998 purchasing power. While this adjustment has the effect of reducing the steepness of the index's path over time, the real-dollar tax index, nevertheless, increased by 139 percent over the period (see table 4.3).

What the Canadian Consumer Tax Index shows

The dramatic increase in the CCTI over the period from 1961 to 1998 was produced by the interaction of a number of factors. First, there was a dramatic increase in incomes over the period and, even with no

Table 4.2: Taxes Paid by the Average Canadian Family (Families and Unattached Individuals), 1961-1998

Year	Average Cash Income ($)	Total Income before Tax ($)	Tax Bill ($)	Increase in tax bill over base year (%)
1961	5,000	7,582	1,675	–
1969	8,000	11,323	3,117	86
1974	12,500	17,976	5,429	224
1976	16,500	21,872	5,979	257
1981	27,980	38,758	11,429	582
1985	32,309	46,451	14,834	786
1990	46,013	64,074	20,413	1,119
1992	46,872	65,717	20,361	1,116
1994	47,257	68,434	21,223	1,167
1996	48,405	70,615	22,681	1,254
1998	49,996	72,695	23,218	1,286

Source: The Fraser Institute, 1998.

Table 4.3: Inflation-Adjusted Tax Bill and Consumer Tax Index, 1961-1998

Year	Tax Bill (1998 $)	Percent change in taxes since 1961
1961	9,719	–
1969	14,453	48.7
1974	18,940	94.9
1976	17,486	79.9
1981	21,054	116.6
1985	21,460	120.8
1990	23,738	144.3
1992	22,092	127.3
1994	22,576	132.3
1996	23,238	139.1
1998	23,218	138.9

Sources: The Fraser Institute, 1998; Statistics Canada, The Consumer Price Index, catalogue 62-001.

change in tax rates, the family's tax bill would have increased substantially: growth in family income alone would have produced an increase in the tax bill from $1,675 in 1961 to $16,749 in 1998. The second contributing factor was a 38.6 percent increase in the tax rate faced by the average family.

Figure 4.2: The Balanced Budget Tax Index, 1961–1998

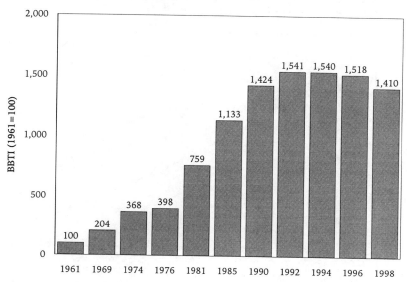

Source: The Fraser Institute.

The increase in the tax burden is even greater when deferred tax-ation, in the form of deficit financing, is included. Figure 4.2 shows what the CCTI looks like when the annual deficits of governments are added to the tax bill. From the mid-1970s until recently, federal and provincial governments resorted to issuing debt to finance a significant portion of their expenditures. Politicians seem finally to have recovered from their infatuation with this form of taxation: the federal govern-ment and many provincial governments have now balanced their bud-gets and all plan to do so by 2001.

What if we got rid of the debt?

A deficit is the amount that government must borrow in any given year to finance spending in excess of taxes. Over the years, these deficits ac-cumulate. This accumulation is known as the debt. All debt must one day be paid off, either by increased taxes or reduced services. There is simply no getting around this fact. Getting rid of deficits is not the same as getting rid of the debt. How would the average Canadian fam-ily's tax index and tax burden change if all levels of government decided to eliminate their debts by the year 2018—20 years from now? Assum-ing a favourable growth rate for real income of 4 percent, population growth of 0.8 percent, and no change in government spending per cap-ita, the average Canadian family's tax bill would rise by $3,453 in the

Figure 4.3: The Impact of Gross Government Debt Repayment on the Average Canadian Family, 1997–2018

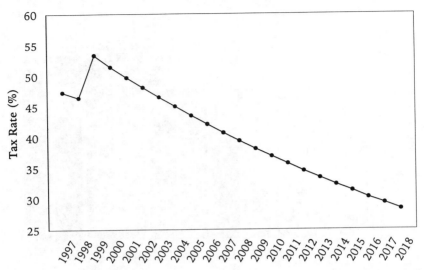

Sources: Statistics Canada; 1998 Federal Budget; calculations by the authors.

first year to pay off the debt within 20 years. The average family's tax rate would jump from 46 percent in 1998 to 53 percent in 1999 and gradually fall to 28 percent in 2018 as seen in figure 4.3.

Taxes versus the necessities of life

While the CCTI shows how the average family's tax bill has changed over the past 37 years, that information becomes even more significant when it is compared with other major expenditures of the average Canadian family for shelter, food, and clothing.

Table 4.4 compares the average dollar amount of family cash income, total income before tax, and total taxes paid with family expenditures on shelter, food, and clothing. Figure 4.4 compares the tax bill to spending on basic needs. It is clear from these figures that taxation has not only become the most significant item that consumers face in their budgets but that it is also growing more rapidly than any other single item. This is made more evident in table 4.5 and figure 4.5, which show the various items as indices based on 1961 values. Total income before tax rose by 859 percent during the period from 1961 to 1998, prices rose by 480 percent, expenditures on shelter by 773 percent, food by 414 percent, and clothing by 387 percent. Meanwhile, the tax bill of the average family grew by 1,286 percent.

Table 4.4: Income, Taxes and Selected Expenditures of the Average Canadian Family (dollars)

Year	Average cash income	Total income before tax	Average tax bill	Average expenditures*		
				Shelter	Food	Clothing
1961	5,000	7,582	1,675	977	1,259	435
1969	8,000	11,323	3,117	1,294	1,634	654
1974	12,500	17,976	5,429	1,983	2,320	886
1976	16,500	21,872	5,979	2,709	2,838	1,119
1981	27,980	38,758	11,429	4,651	4,440	1,499
1985	32,309	46,451	14,834	6,036	4,899	2,141
1990	46,013	64,074	20,413	7,791	5,947	2,417
1992	46,872	65,717	20,361	8,500	6,189	2,325
1994	47,257	68,434	21,223	8,494	6,210	2,210
1996	48,405	70,615	22,681	8,487	6,231	2,095
1998	49,996	72,695	23,218	8,528	6,466	2,120

Sources: Statistics Canada, Urban Family Expenditure, catalogue 62-549, 62-547, 62-544, 62-537, 62-535, 62-541, 62-525, 62-555; 1990, 1992, and 1996 Family Expenditure Surveys, catalogue 62-555; The Consumer Price Index, 62-001; The Fraser Institute, 1998.

* All expenditure items include indirect taxes.

Figure 4.4: Taxes and Basic Expenditures of the Average Canadian Family, 1961–1998

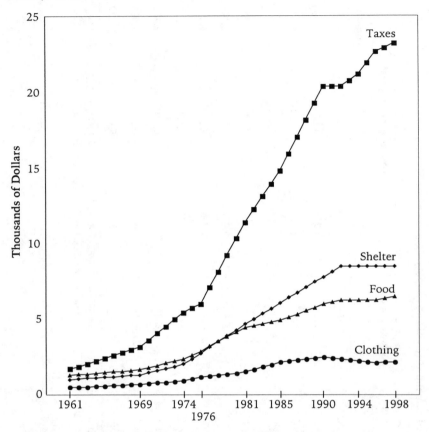

Source: Table 4.4. Note that all expenditure items include indirect taxes. Years noted are those for which there is actual data.

Table 4.6 and figure 4.6 present the same information as above expressed as a percentage of total income before tax. Total income before tax is a broader measure of income than cash income since it includes non-cash items such as interest accumulated on pension fund income but not cashed by the recipient. In this form, the data reveal some interesting comparisons. For example:

- In 1961, the average family had to use 35 percent of its income to provide itself with shelter, food, and clothing. In the same year, 22 percent of the family's income went to government as tax.

Table 4.5: Income, Tax, and Expenditure Indices (1961=100)

Year	Income		Tax	Consumer Prices	Selected expenditures (All expenditure items include indirect taxes.)		
	Average cash income	Total income before tax	CCTI	Average CPI	Average shelter	Average food	Average clothing
1961	100	100	100	100	100	100	100
1969	160	149	186	125	132	130	150
1974	250	237	324	166	203	184	204
1976	330	288	357	198	277	225	257
1981	560	511	682	315	476	353	345
1985	646	613	886	401	618	389	492
1990	920	845	1,219	499	797	472	556
1992	937	867	1,216	535	870	492	535
1994	945	903	1,267	545	869	493	508
1996	968	931	1,354	566	869	495	482
1998	1,000	959	1,386	580	873	514	487
Percentage increase 1961–1998							
	900	859	1,286	480	773	414	387

Sources: Table 4.4; Statistics Canada, Consumer Price Index, 62-001. All figures in this table are converted to indices by dividing each series in table 4.4 by its value in 1961, and then multiplying that figure by 100.

Figure 4.5: How the Canadian Consumer Tax Index (CCTI) Has Increased Relative to Other Indices, 1961–1998

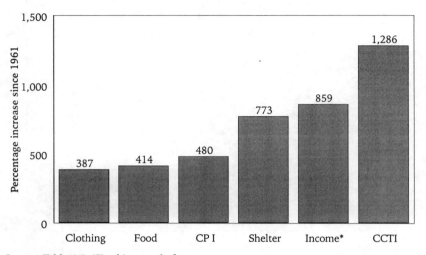

Source: Table 4.5. *Total income before tax.

Table 4.6: Taxes and Expenditures of the Average Canadian Family (percentage of total income before tax)

Year	Taxes	Expenditures		
		Shelter	Food	Clothing
1961	22.1	12.9	16.6	5.7
1969	27.5	11.4	14.4	5.8
1974	30.2	11.0	12.9	4.9
1976	27.3	12.4	13.0	5.1
1981	29.5	12.0	11.5	3.9
1985	31.9	13.0	10.5	4.6
1990	31.9	12.2	9.3	3.8
1992	31.0	12.9	9.4	3.5
1994	31.0	12.4	9.1	3.2
1996	32.1	12.0	8.8	3.0
1998	31.9	11.7	8.9	2.9
Source: Table 4.5.				

Figure 4.6: Taxes and Expenditures of the Average Canadian Family (percentage of total income before tax)

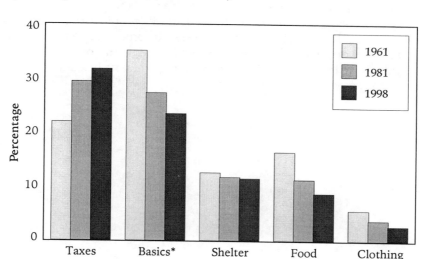

Source: Table 4.6. *Sum of shelter, food, and clothing.

- By 1974, the situation had been reversed and 30 percent of income was taken by government in the form of taxes, while only 29 percent was used to provide the family with shelter, food, and clothing.

- By 1998, the situation had become worse. Whereas the proportion of income consumed by taxes had continued to increase, the fraction of income spent on necessities (shelter, food, and clothing) had dropped dramatically. The average family spent 23.5 percent of its income on the necessities of life while 32 percent of its income went to taxes.

- The sum of taxes and spending on necessities accounts for 55 to 60 percent of total income before tax for all the years shown, with taxes representing a much larger share than in 1961.

Tax Freedom Day

The CCTI is only one tool for evaluating the Canadian tax system. Another easily understood and revealing measure is the Tax Freedom Day of the average Canadian family. The average Canadian family is the family whose income is the average income of all families with two or more members. Tax Freedom Day (TFD) is that day of the year when the average family has done enough work to pay the total tax bill imposed on it by the federal, provincial, and municipal governments. It is calculated as the percentage of cash income the family pays in tax multiplied by 365 days to arrive at the number of days of work required to pay the total tax bill. If 50 percent of one's income goes to taxes, then one must work one-half the year for government, and one's TFD falls on July 2. In 1961, TFD fell on May 3. Since then, it has advanced 55 days, so that in 1998 it fell on June 27.

Chapter 5
The Relative Tax Burden

THE FIRST THING people ask about the tax system is: How much do I pay? Tax Freedom Day and the Canadian Consumer Tax Index discussed in the last chapter give a rough answer to this query. The next thing people want to know is how much are others paying? Are some paying less than others? These are more complicated questions because they call for a broad view of what the tax system does. Some in the media and many social activist groups believe these questions have a clear and simple answer: the "rich" pay no taxes and the poor are getting "shafted by the system." In this chapter, we suggest that the answers are not so simple. We look at all income groups and how their relative income and tax positions have changed between 1961 and 1998. A reasonable analysis of these numbers points to a different conclusion than the one presented by groups that claim Canada's tax system needs to be more progressive than it is.

The distribution of income

In order to analyze the relative income and tax positions of Canadians, we have divided all Canadian families into three broad income groups based on income deciles. The first income decile is one of ten groups that result from arranging families according to their total income before tax, from lowest to highest, and then selecting the ten percent of families with the lowest incomes; the second decile is the next ten percent of families, and so on. The lowest income group includes the families in the bottom three deciles; the middle group includes the next four deciles; the upper group includes the top three deciles. The resulting groups are presented in table 5.1 and illustrated in figure 5.1.

47

Table 5.1: Decile Distribution of Income (income before tax)

Year	Income groups		
	Lower 3 deciles (%)	Middle 4 deciles (%)	Upper 3 deciles (%)
1961	10.8	35.6	53.6
1972	9.0	33.1	57.9
1976	8.8	31.7	59.5
1981	10.0	34.9	55.0
1985	10.2	35.1	54.7
1990	8.7	33.9	57.4
1992	8.9	33.0	58.1
1994	9.1	33.3	57.6
1996	9.2	33.3	57.5
1998	9.2	33.4	57.4

Source: The Fraser Institute, 1998.

Table 5.1 reveals that the relative shares of the different income groups have been remarkably constant over the period from 1961 through 1998. A note of caution: in evaluating this result, the reader should bear in mind that a number of aspects of the data make them suscepti- ble to misinterpretation. First, the data fail to make any allowance for

Figure 5.1: Percent of Total Income before Tax Earned by Each Income Group, 1961–1998

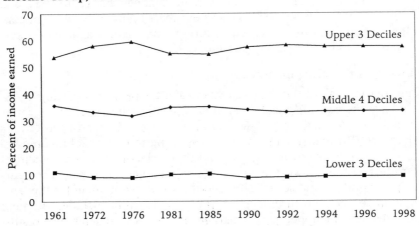

Source: The Fraser Institute, 1998.

Table 5.2: Income in Age Groups as a Percentage of Average for All Age Groups, Canadian Males, 1996

Age	Revenue Canada taxation statistics (%)	Statistics Canada income survey data (%)	Mixed profile (%)
<25	32.6	50.8	41.7
25–34	86.0	95.5	90.7
35–44	120.0	121.8	120.9
45–54	137.1	137.2	137.2
55–65	120.8	115.2	118.0
>65	86.8	79.5	83.2

Source: Statistics Canada, Income Distribution by Size in Canada 1996, catalogue number 13-207; Revenue Canada, Tax Statistics on Individuals, 1993 Tax Year (Interim Statistics-Universe Data); calculations by the authors.

the age of individuals. This is important, since age is a principal determinant of income. Young people first entering the labour market typically earn wages or salaries considerably below the average and considerably below what will be their own lifetime average. Similarly, those who have passed the age of retirement are typically in a phase of their life when their incomes are considerably below their lifetime average and when they are spending the savings and pensions accumulated from their working lifetimes.

To illustrate this point, table 5.2 displays the "life-cycle average expected wage" for a Canadian male in 1996. Two sources of data on the earnings profile are available: information from Revenue Canada's *Tax Statistics*, and Statistics Canada's income surveys. While the two sources yield different estimates, they both show the large fluctuations in income relative to the average that one is likely to experience throughout one's life.

Failure to account for the age of income earners can lead to a considerably distorted impression of how income distribution is changing because there have been dramatic changes in the age structure of the population in Canada. Birth rates have declined and mortality rates have decreased since the 1960s. In 1966, the ratio of Canadians under 20 to Canadians over 65 was 5.5 to 1. This ratio decreased to 2.3 by 1995, and is expected to decline further to 1.1 by the year 2030. In future years, as the number of people retired or nearing retirement grows, we can expect that the distribution of income will be affected. More of the population will be elderly and more of the population will have lower incomes as a result. This will not mean, however, that the population is, in a real sense, worse off.

A second important warning for those who would draw conclusions from these data about the equity of the income distribution is that they ignore income-in-kind that people receive from government. Housing, medical care, education, and other services that are received as direct benefits from government rather than as cash payments are not reflected in the income distribution. The public provision of these services represents one of the most substantial redistributive aspects of Canadian society.

For these reasons it would be inappropriate to infer from the data in table 5.1 that there had been no change in the effective distribution of income since 1961. The data in their present form are incapable of providing meaningful answers to that question. What the data do provide is a yardstick against which to measure the distribution of taxes. This yardstick will allow us to infer whether, for example, groups of people with low incomes bear a disproportionate share of the tax burden. It will provide an indication of the progressivity or regressivity of the Canadian tax burden. In order to arrive at these results, it is necessary to combine income results with those on tax distribution.

Tax distribution and tax rates

Our measurements of the distribution of the tax burden provide some interesting and, indeed, puzzling results. Whereas up until the mid-1970s there had been a more or less steady increase in the total tax burden borne by the upper third of income groups, from 1976 to 1981 the share of the top group fell markedly. As table 5.3 and figure 5.2 indicate, during 1976 families in the top three income deciles accounted

Table 5.3: Decile Distribution of Taxes (percent)

Year	Lower 3 deciles (%)	Middle 4 deciles (%)	Upper 3 deciles (%)
1961	8.7	30.6	60.9
1972	6.0	30.0	64.0
1976	6.1	27.3	66.5
1981	6.8	33.3	59.9
1985	7.1	33.6	59.4
1990	5.5	31.7	62.8
1992	4.9	30.2	64.9
1994	5.0	30.4	64.7
1996	5.0	30.6	64.4
1998	5.1	30.9	64.0

Source: The Fraser Institute, 1998.

Figure 5.2: Percent of Total Taxes Paid by Each Income Group, 1961–1998

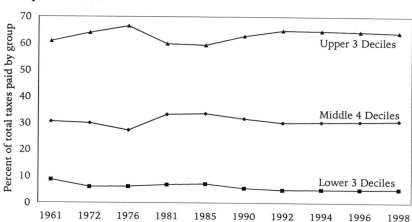

Source: The Fraser Institute, 1998.

for fully 66.5 percent of the total tax payments. By 1981, this had fallen to 59.9 percent of the total, a decrease of 6.6 percentage points. The decline in the tax burden borne by the top three income deciles was nearly matched by a corresponding increase in the tax burden faced by those in the middle income deciles. For example, families in the fourth to seventh income deciles, which had borne 27.3 percent of the total tax burden in 1976, were bearing 33.3 percent by 1981, an increase of 6.0 percentage points. Between 1981 and 1992, the share of the total tax burden paid by the top income group increased and, since 1992, has been falling slightly. In contrast, between 1981 and 1992 the share paid by the middle four deciles dropped and, since 1992, has been increasing slightly.

The income tax paid by the upper income group has been rising since 1985 while that paid by the lower two income groups has been decreasing. As table 5.4 shows, there had been a modest shift in the incidence of the personal income tax system away from the upper income deciles and toward the lower income deciles until the early and mid-1980s. This was reversed in the late 1980s and early 1990s. The top three income groups accounted for 62.7 percent of total income tax payments in 1981, down from 68.1 percent in 1976. By 1998, the top three income deciles accounted for 69.4 percent of total income tax payments.

A major factor explaining variations in the share of taxes paid by the top three deciles has been the change in the incidence of capital-related taxes. These are chiefly property taxes and taxes on

Table 5.4: Decile Distribution of Personal Income Taxes (percent)

Year	Lower 3 deciles (%)	Middle 4 deciles (%)	Upper 3 deciles (%)
1976	3.2	29.5	68.1
1981	4.4	32.9	62.7
1985	4.5	34.3	61.2
1990	3.8	31.0	65.2
1992	2.9	27.3	69.8
1994	2.9	27.1	69.9
1996	2.9	27.3	69.8
1998	3.1	27.5	69.4

Source: The Fraser Institute, 1998.

corporate profits. As table 5.5 reveals, there have been relatively large fluctuations in the pattern of these capital-related taxes. Between 1976 and 1981, the burden of profit taxes for the top three deciles dropped from 72.2 to 66.9 percent. The burden crept up to 71.8 percent in 1985 and fell to 62.0 percent in 1998.

Analysis of the underlying factors reveals that part of the reason for the dramatic shift in the incidence of capital taxes has been the change in the distribution of capital income amongst Canadians (see table 5.6). Changes in exemptions are another probable reason why capital taxes fell for the upper income deciles in the late 1970s and early 1980s, then rose in the late 1980s. For example, in the early 1980s Canadians took advantage of the tax preferences that the government inserted in the tax system to encourage the development of various sectors of the economy, such as oil exploration, rental housing, and Canadian films. The tax reform of 1987 effectively put an end to much of the tax preference game. The recent growth in capital income taxes in the lower and middle deciles may be due to the growth in the value of the stock market and increases in the number of people holding stocks through their mutual funds.

One factor that underlies all of the distribution series is the massive surge in the number of families in the upper income classes. In 1980, for example, only 26.0 percent of families had an income of $35,000 or more. By 1996, 68.3 percent of families enjoyed an income at least as large as that. While inflation has played a large role in this development, some of the increase in the number of families in the higher income groups is the result of the fact that an increasing number of families contain two income earners whose joint income pushes the family into the higher tax bracket.

Table 5.5: Decile Distribution of Profit Taxes and Property Taxes (percent)

Year	Profit taxes		
	Lower 3 deciles (%)	Middle 4 deciles (%)	Upper 3 deciles (%)
1976	10.3	17.8	72.2
1981	9.1	24.0	66.9
1985	6.7	21.6	71.8
1990	5.8	24.5	69.7
1992	7.4	27.6	65.1
1994	7.0	27.4	65.7
1996	7.3	28.2	64.5
1998	8.0	30.1	62.0

Year	Property taxes		
	Lower 3 deciles (%)	Middle 4 deciles (%)	Upper 3 deciles (%)
1976	10.3	17.8	72.2
1981	10.9	26.8	62.3
1985	6.6	21.6	71.8
1990	5.7	24.4	69.9
1992	7.0	26.9	66.1
1994	6.8	27.0	66.2
1996	7.1	27.8	65.1
1998	8.0	30.0	62.0

Source: The Fraser Institute, 1998.

Table 5.6: Decile Distribution of Capital Income (percent)

Year	Lower 3 deciles (%)	Middle 4 deciles (%)	Upper 3 deciles (%)
1976	10.3	17.8	72.2
1981	9.1	23.9	66.9
1985	6.8	22.0	71.2
1990	5.9	24.9	69.3
1992	7.4	27.6	65.1
1994	7.1	27.6	65.4
1996	7.4	28.3	64.3
1998	8.2	30.4	61.5

Source: The Fraser Institute, 1998.

The implication of this increase in the number of families with two income earners for the distribution of taxation amongst families is that the upper income deciles seem to be paying less and less tax because they are composed increasingly of individuals with lower incomes. As noted in chapter 2, two incomes totaling, say, $30,000 are taxed less in total than one income of $30,000. Since upper income families are increasingly composed of two income earners, this has put downward pressure on the average tax rate in this income range.

Consequently, from 1976 until 1985 the percentage of total income earned by the upper income groups had been steadily decreasing while the middle and lower income groups gained ground. This is quite clearly reflected in Table 5.1, which shows the distribution of income by decile. Whereas in 1976 nearly 60 percent of all income was earned by those in the top three deciles, this had dropped to 54.7 percent by 1985. However, by 1998 the upper three deciles had rebounded to claim 57.4 percent of income. Whether or not this is the start of a new trend is too early to tell. One further implication of the distribution of total taxes is interesting to note: figure 5.2 shows that the decline in progressivity in the tax system that began to emerge in the late 1970s was reversed by 1985.

A look across the generations

The tables on income distribution presented above give only a snapshot of the number of Canadians who fall into various income groups at one point in time. We must look at these tables with an understanding of what they can and cannot tell us. These tables are perfectly adequate for showing that our tax system is progressive and how much current upper income groups pay versus current lower income groups. What these tables do not show is that while there is a fairly constant proportion of the population in these income groups, the composition of these groups changes significantly from year to year. What this means is that there is not a "permanent underclass" stuck in the lower income group.

From lifetime income and tax simulations done for previous editions of this book we know that the average lifetime tax rate is higher than the average tax rate from the snapshot. We also know that there is less inequality in average lifetime tax rates than suggested by the snapshot. This should come as no surprise in light of the fact that many young families start out in the low income group and work up to the middle or high income group. There is less inequality in the long term because many families will initially have low income and low taxes followed by middle income and middle taxes and possibly high income and high taxes as they move through their life cycles.

Table 5.7: People Classified by Their Family Income Quintile in 1993 and 1994 (thousands)

		Income quintile in 1994				
		First (bottom)	Second	Third	Fourth	Fifth (top)
Income quintile in 1993	First (bottom)	3,818	1,160	235	100	43
	Second	910	3,033	1,077	251	86
	Third	272	817	3,105	1,046	143
	Fourth	165	301	768	3,233	918
	Fifth (top)	134	122	200	728	4,199

Source: Statistics Canada, *Crossing The Low Income Line*, product number 75F0002M, 1997.

Evidence of just how much the composition of income groups fluctuates has recently been released from Statistics Canada's Survey of Labour and Income Dynamics. Table 5.7 presents the shifts in a group of people's position in the overall income distribution between 1993 and 1994. This table shows that there were 3.105 million people in the third income quintile in both 1993 and 1994, that 1.046 million who were in the third quintile in 1993 had moved up to the fourth in 1994, and that 0.817 million people dropped from the third to the second quintile between 1993 and 1994.

More generally, table 5.7 shows that between 1993 and 1994

- 64.7 percent of families did not change quintile

- 15.6 percent moved up one quintile

- 12.0 percent dropped one quintile

- 3.2 percent moved up more than one quintile

- 4.4 percent dropped more than one quintile

Who pays the tax bill?

Table 5.3 shows that the largest portion of the tax burden ultimately settles on the higher income groups. In 1998, the top 30 percent of families earned 57.4 of all income in Canada and paid 64.0 percent of all taxes. The bottom 30 percent earned 9.2 percent of all income and paid 5.1 percent of all taxes.

To economists these figures are nothing out of the ordinary. Our tax system is progressive. It is not surprising to find that those earning lower income pay less taxes as a proportion of their income than those earning higher income. This result may, however, come as surprise to activists and reporters who claim that the "rich" in Canada pay no taxes. As tables 5.3 and 5.4 show, the rich bear *most* of Canada's taxation burden. Some critics might counter that the rich in Canada avoid taxes by holding their wealth in corporations and that corporations can avoid taxes better than individuals. We address this question in chapter 7 and present the results of a study done by the Ontario government's Fair Tax Commission, which found that corporations do pay their taxes.

Who belongs to the club of the top 30 percent of Canadian families? A Canadian family is included in the top 30 percent when its cash income exceeds $60,113. The average income in this group is $96,443.

Get it from the rich

It is often said—and all too often believed—that the key to "social welfare" or "social justice" is the redistribution of income. That is, the state should take income from those who have more and give it to those who have less. The extreme form of this prescription is "from each according to his ability [to pay] and to each according to his need"—the rule advanced in the Communist Manifesto (Marx and Engels 1848).

The preceding section's analysis of who pays the income tax reveals that as a country, Canada already engages in significant taxation of those who are relatively well-off. It remains interesting, therefore, to inquire whether or not we could achieve a more equal distribution of the benefits of the Canadian good life by taxing more of the income of the richest Canadians.

How rich is rich?

The question that immediately arises is "How rich is rich?" At what income level should the government tax away all increases in the interest of "equitable" income distribution? For the sake of illustration, let us choose the income at which a family moves from the middle 4 deciles of income to the upper 3 deciles as the maximum income that Canadians should be allowed to earn. Under this rule, all incomes above $60,113 would be subject to a 100 percent rate of income tax and the proceeds would be distributed to all income earners with incomes less than $60,113.

Counting the rich

In 1996, 1,512,320 persons filed tax returns reporting an income of $60,000 or more. Note that, in this section, individual and not family incomes are the focus of the analysis. Total income reported by these people was $154 billion. If the government had really taxed away all income beyond $60,000, the total tax revenue in 1996 would have been $20.1 billion higher than it actually was. Redistribution of this increased tax revenue to those 18.9 million tax filers with incomes less than $60,000 would yield an average annual payment of $1,065 for each person submitting a tax return.

Taxing the "rich" is not the source of wealth

This calculation is important because it reveals the practical impossibility of "getting it from the rich and redistributing it to the poor." A look back to table 2.6 reveals that only 7.4 percent of tax filers earned more than $60,000 in 1996. Those who are impatient with the speed at which the economic process improves the condition of the poorest members of society ought to reflect on the fact that the same total increase in the incomes of those earning less than $60,000 would be achieved by about a 5.2 percent growth in total incomes, even if it were distributed in exactly the same way as it is now. What Canada needs are more "rich" people; imposing more taxes is not the way to increase anyone's wealth.

The rags-to-riches tax burden

In the previous sections we have shown in general terms how our progressive tax system imposes ever increasing burdens on people as they earn more income. What about an individual who had started off in 1961 with meagre earnings and had brought himself up in the ranks? What kind of message does our tax system send to this person? Table 5.8 presents the results of a tax analysis for such an individual. We assume that when he started working in 1961 he was earning $2,750 a year in cash income, half the average income, and that his income grew steadily and at such a rate that by 1998 he was earning twice the average, or $99,990 a year.

Table 5.8: The Rags-to-Riches Tax Burden

	1961	1969	1976	1981	1990	1998	Percentage increase 1961–1998
Cash income ($)	2,750	5,981	11,804	19,183	45,975	99,990	3,536
Total income before tax ($)	4,775	9,925	18,827	29,743	67,744	140,812	2,849
Taxes paid($)	960	2,263	4,791	8,188	21,481	50,630	5,174
Taxes as a percentage of total income before tax (%)	20.1	22.8	25.4	27.5	31.7	36.0	78.8
Source: The Fraser Institute, 1998.							

In 1961, this person's total income before tax of $4,775 attracted a tax bill of $960, or an average tax rate of total income of 20.1 percent. By 1976, the hypothetical income earner had a total income before tax of $18,827 and paid taxes of $4,791, for a tax rate of 25.4 percent. Finally, in 1998, when his cash income was $99,990, his total income before tax was $140,812, and his taxes paid amounted to $50,630. Thus, the average tax rate on total income before tax had risen from 20.1 to 36.0 percent.

Over the period of 37 years from 1961 to 1998, our hypothetical income earner experienced a 2,849 percent increase in total income before tax. Over the same period, his taxes paid increased by 5,174 percent and taxes as a percentage of total income before tax increased by 78.8 percent.

Marginal versus average tax rates

The tax rate that one earns on the next dollar of income is referred to as the "marginal tax rate." It can differ dramatically from the average tax rate, which is the rate that we are most accustomed to thinking about. Table 5.9 shows both marginal and average rates for different income levels; figure 5.3 illustrates them.

It is this marginal rate that enters into people's decisions about how much to work. When someone decides whether or not to work an extra hour, she asks herself how much extra she will earn and how much extra tax she will pay. She does not consider how much tax on average she is paying because this does not reflect the true return to any extra effort she may wish to provide. As table 5.9 shows, these rates jump considerably as one moves from the second to the third income decile, reflecting that initially it is very costly to work because one rapidly loses social assistance. The reason for this result is that many social assistance payments are reduced (the gains are "clawed back") once the recipient starts earning income. In effect, these "claw-backs" can cause the tax rate on the first few dollars of earned income to be very high. This effect fades in the middle income brackets but rises again at higher levels of income from the effect of increasing progressivity.

Table 5.9: Average and Marginal Tax Rates, 1998

Average tax rates (percent)									
Lower income groups			Middle income groups				Upper income groups		
1	2	3	4	5	6	7	8	9	10
Income measure = cash income									
13.0%	21.3%	30.7%	38.2%	43.6%	46.8%	48.1%	50.4%	52.1%	60.6%
Income measure = total income before tax									
10.4%	16.7%	22.6%	26.9%	30.2%	32.1%	33.1%	34.3%	35.7%	39.8%

Marginal tax rates (percent) faced when moving from a lower to a higher decile									
	1 to 2	2 to 3	3 to 4	4 to 5	5 to 6	6 to 7	7 to 8	8 to 9	9 to 10
Income measure = cash income									
	28.8%	56.9%	67.8%	66.5%	63.4%	55.1%	62.2%	59.1%	72.7%
Income measure = total income before tax									
	22.0%	35.9%	41.1%	43.2%	41.4%	38.2%	40.6%	41.3%	45.1%
Source: The Fraser Institute, 1998.									

Figure 5.3: Average and Marginal Tax Rates by Income Decile, 1998

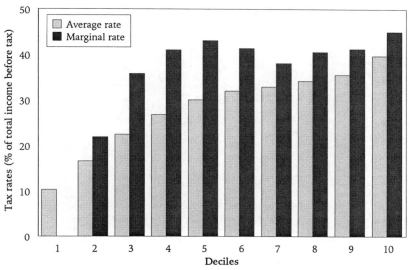

Source: The Fraser Institute, 1998.

Chapter 6
Taxes across Canada

TAXES ARE THE PRICE one pays for government services. If taxes were the same in all provinces, the first five chapters of this book would be a sufficient price guide to government services. As provinces differ in their taxes, however, we need to break our analysis down by province. This breakdown may be of interest to Canadians who want an idea of where taxes are lightest and where they are heaviest. It may also be of interest to government officials who understand that it is dangerous for the economic health of a province when it imposes significantly more tax than its neighbours. Figure 6.1 shows the tax rate as a percent of cash income for the average Canadian family by province.

Figure 6.1: Tax Rates of the Average Family, 1998

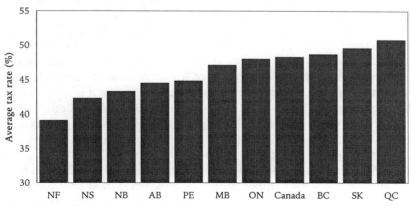

Source: The Fraser Institute, 1998.

In comparing the provinces, we must make some adjustment for the fact that family size differs among provinces. The family whose income is average in Newfoundland has more members than its counterpart in Ontario. Put differently, Newfoundland has relatively fewer single-member families than does Ontario. We would not be comparing the same sort of family if we set these averages side by side. To get a more precise comparison, this chapter focuses on families of two or more individuals. However, the appendix shows that many of the results hold for families and unattached individuals, and families of two parents with two children under the age of 18.

Different strokes

Table 6.1 presents the tax situation for the average family by province of residence. In this context, "average family" means a family unit that has an average income in its province of residence. Thus, for example, the average family in Newfoundland had a cash income of $47,655 in 1998 whereas the average family in Ontario had an income of $67,060 in the same year, and so on. Table 6.2 shows which provinces have the highest propensity to tax in each of the tax categories. Income tax comprises between 32.8 percent and 41.1 percent of the family's tax bill. The highest rate comes from Alberta, where the average family provides 41.1 percent of its taxes in income tax. The lowest proportion is in Saskatchewan, at 32.8 percent. The sales tax is most heavily relied upon in the Maritimes. For instance, 19.2 cents out of each tax dollar paid in taxes by the average Newfoundland family are collected in sales tax. By comparison, 16.3 cents out of each tax dollar are collected in sales tax from the average Quebec family, while just 7.9 cents per tax dollar are collected from that source from the average Albertan family, as Alberta has no provincial sales tax. Ontario has the highest reliance on property tax, collecting 8.7 percent of taxes in this form, whereas Newfoundland only collects 3.4 percent of its taxes as property tax.

Saskatchewan, Alberta, and British Columbia are the only provinces that have significant natural-resource revenues. In Alberta, for example, petroleum-related taxes are not collected from the tax paying public; rather, they are collected from the corporations that remove oil and gas from the ground. It is nevertheless the case that the oil and gas in the ground in Alberta belongs to the people of Alberta. Since they do not receive the income from these natural resources, it is appropriate to regard the taxes that are paid as a result of exploitation of these petroleum resources as a tax on Albertans.

While this is the appropriate technical treatment of petroleum resource taxes, however, apportioning these taxes in this way does confuse somewhat the inter-provincial comparison of tax burdens. If we

Table 6.1: Taxes of the Average Canadian Family (with two or more individuals), 1998 (dollars)

	Average cash income	Average total income before tax	Income tax	Sales tax	Amusement taxes*	Automobile taxes**	Payroll taxes***	Property tax	Import duties	Profits tax	Natural resource taxes	Other taxes	Total taxes
NF	47,655	65,586	7,410	3,574	1,697	888	2,657	,641	145	874	100	665	18,652
PE	48,400	70,683	7,634	4,386	1,720	932	3,480	1,417	215	1,527	9	387	21,707
NS	52,486	74,862	8,868	4,158	1,896	895	3,618	1,108	199	1,219	21	203	22,186
NB	53,492	76,793	9,041	4,443	1,858	1,037	3,512	1,434	208	1,157	117	355	23,162
QC	54,210	78,769	10,667	4,492	1,579	888	5,487	1,872	229	1,964	55	285	27,517
ON	67,060	98,557	11,783	5,610	1,973	992	5,571	2,791	290	2,608	44	552	32,215
MB	60,187	87,941	10,597	4,759	2,379	862	4,390	1,660	263	1,885	65	1,494	28,354
SK	54,490	83,154	8,876	4,320	2,341	1,473	3,772	2,053	231	2,447	911	628	27,053
AB	65,897	96,255	12,053	2,301	2,474	832	5,306	1,649	275	2,133	1,336	954	29,314
BC	60,671	88,973	11,003	4,786	2,091	751	4,843	1,820	271	2,211	777	995	29,548
Canada	60,928	89,140	11,128	4,775	1,953	,93	5,171	2,148	260	2,208	280	597	29,455

Source: The Fraser Institute, 1998.
*Amusement taxes include liquor, tobacco, amusement, and other excise taxes.
**Automobile taxes include Automobile, fuel, and motor vehicle license taxes.
***Payroll taxes include social security, pension, medical, and hospital taxes.

Table 6.2: Individual Taxes as a Proportion of the Total Tax Bill for the Average Family (with two or more individuals), 1998 (percent)

	Income tax	Sales tax	Amusement taxes*	Automobile taxes**	Payroll taxes***	Property tax	Import duties	Profits tax	Natural resource taxes	Other taxes
NF	39.7	19.2	9.1	4.8	14.2	3.4	0.8	4.7	0.5	3.6
PE	35.2	20.2	7.9	4.3	16.0	6.5	1.0	7.0	0.0	1.8
NS	40.0	18.7	8.5	4.0	16.3	5.0	0.9	5.5	0.1	0.9
NB	39.0	19.2	8.0	4.5	15.2	6.2	0.9	5.0	0.5	1.5
QC	38.8	16.3	5.7	3.2	19.9	6.8	0.8	7.1	0.2	1.0
ON	36.6	17.4	6.1	3.1	17.3	8.7	0.9	8.1	0.1	1.7
MB	37.4	16.8	8.4	3.0	15.5	5.9	0.9	6.6	0.2	5.3
SK	32.8	16.0	8.7	5.4	13.9	7.6	0.9	9.0	3.4	2.3
AB	41.1	7.9	8.4	2.8	18.1	5.6	0.9	7.3	4.6	3.3
BC	37.2	16.2	7.1	2.5	16.4	6.2	0.9	7.5	2.6	3.4
Canada	37.8	16.2	6.6	3.2	17.6	7.3	0.9	7.5	1.0	2.0

Source: The Fraser Institute, 1998.
*Amusement taxes include liquor, tobacco, amusement, and other excise taxes.
**Automobile taxes include Automobile, fuel, and motor vehicle license taxes.
***Payroll taxes include social security, pension, medical, and hospital taxes.

subtracted from the $29,314 total tax bill faced by the average Albertan family the $1,336 collected on their behalf from the petroleum industry, we find that the total tax bill is reduced to $27,978 for the average family. Without natural-resource taxes, the tax bill for Saskatchewan and British Columbia would be $26,142 and $28,771, respectively. Table 6.3 presents the tax rates for the average family with, and without natural resource levies for the provinces that have significant revenues from this tax source.

In comparing the tax results for the various provinces, it is important to remember that the standard of comparison is the average family, the family in each province whose income is average. Since the average income in each province varies considerably, some of the differences in the tax burden among the provinces is due to nothing more than differences in income.

Table 6.4 provides a distribution of taxes by province according to income deciles. The great benefit of this table is that it makes possible a comparison of the provinces according to how the tax burden is distributed amongst the various income groups within each province. The outcome of this analysis, as reflected in the table, is remarkable; there is little variation among the provinces in the extent of the progressivity or regressivity of their various tax systems. The upper income groups in all provinces absorb between 62 and 71 percent of the total tax bill.

The similarity of the tax distributions in the provinces is noteworthy because it exists in spite of the differences in the provincial tax systems. These differences, which were pointed out above in the discussion of table 6.1, ought to provide some variation in the tax rates unless, as is apparent from table 6.4, the differences in the progressivity and regressivity of the various taxes largely offset one other.

There are, however, some important differences between the tax systems in the various provinces. Table 6.5 highlights the differences in average tax rates payable by the various income deciles in each province. Thus, in Newfoundland for example, the lowest income decile paid a tax rate of 6.3 percent on average whereas the top decile paid a tax rate of 41.2 percent. In Saskatchewan, on the other hand, the bottom decile paid 17.1 percent while the top decile paid 38.6 percent.

Underlying this pattern of taxation is a pattern of government expenditures: the reason for raising revenues is to pay for government spending. Accordingly, an alternative, and perhaps more direct, measure of the level of government activity is the level of government spending. Table 6.6 presents both the total amounts and the per-capita amounts of provincial government spending in each of the provinces, adjusted for the amount of that spending that is financed by federal equalization payments.

Table 6.3: Provincial Tax Rates for an Average Family with Two
or More Individuals, 1998 (percent)

	Taxes to cash income	Taxes to total income before tax
Newfoundland	39.1	28.4
Prince Edward Island	44.8	30.7
Nova Scotia	42.3	29.6
New Brunswick	43.3	30.2
Quebec	50.8	34.9
Ontario	48.0	32.7
Manitoba	47.1	32.2
Saskatchewan	49.6	32.5
Alberta	44.5	30.5
British Columbia	48.7	33.2
Canada	48.3	33.0
Tax Rates Excluding Natural Resources Taxes		
Saskatchewan	48.0	31.4
Alberta	42.5	29.1
British Columbia	47.4	32.3
Canada	47.9	32.7

Source: The Fraser Institute, 1998.

Table 6.4: Decile Distribution of Taxes by Province, 1998 (percent)

	Lower 3 deciles	Middle 4 deciles	Upper 3 deciles
Newfoundland	2.5	26.8	70.6
Prince Edward Island	4.0	30.8	65.2
Nova Scotia	4.4	29.5	66.1
New Brunswick	3.2	29.9	66.9
Quebec	5.8	31.8	62.4
Ontario	6.0	31.2	62.8
Manitoba	4.2	28.2	67.7
Saskatchewan	5.5	29.0	65.4
Alberta	4.4	30.0	65.6
British Columbia	4.4	30.5	65.1
Canada	5.1	30.9	64.0

Source: The Fraser Institute, 1998.

Table 6.5: Average Tax Rates* by Decile and Province, 1998 (percent)

Decile	Lower income groups			Middle income groups				Upper income groups		
	1	2	3	4	5	6	7	8	9	10
NF	6.3	5.2	12.2	15.7	21.3	27.0	31.2	33.8	37.0	41.2
PE	8.8	9.6	14.7	19.6	24.4	27.8	'29.1	31.2	32.8	33.5
NS	9.5	13.1	17.8	22.1	25.8	28.9	30.2	32.1	33.4	38.2
NB	8.1	9.1	14.7	21.1	25.6	28.3	30.9	32.0	33.7	38.3
QC	12.9	18.7	23.0	28.1	30.9	33.9	36.0	37.4	38.4	42.6
ON	10.9	19.9	24.9	28.7	30.8	31.8	32.9	33.7	34.9	40.0
MB	9.9	11.4	19.4	22.5	26.1	30.6	30.7	32.6	35.3	41.4
SK	17.1	12.9	22.9	24.4	26.9	30.2	30.6	33.1	33.2	38.6
AB	9.2	13.3	18.9	23.7	27.8	29.6	30.6	32.0	33.0	36.4
BC	10.3	14.6	22.3	27.6	30.9	32.6	32.9	34.1	36.3	40.5
Canada	10.4	16.7	22.6	26.9	30.2	32.1	33.1	34.3	35.7	39.8

Source: The Fraser Institute, 1998; *using total income before tax.

Table 6.6: Provincial Government Spending, 1998/99

	Total spending ($millions)	Per Person Figures			Rank by spending	Rank by taxation
		Total spending ($)	Federal transfers ($)	Spending net of transfers ($)		
NF	3,043	5,487	2,411	3,076	9	10
PE	782	5,723	2,107	3,616	8	6
NS	4,513	4,769	1,803	2,966	10	9
NB	4,464	5,872	2,063	3,809	6	8
QC	41,842	5,617	818	4,798	1	1
ON	56,964	4,942	432	4,509	4	4
MB	5,736	5,021	1,393	3,627	7	5
SK	5,233	5,118	817	4,301	5	2
AB	14,955	5,170	448	4,723	2	7
BC	20,536	5,188	476	4,711	3	3

Source: Provincial budgets; calculations by authors.

Table 6.6 reveals an interesting pattern of spending, especially when compared with the taxation data. The data reveal that Quebec and British Columbia are among the provinces that spend the most and tax the most while the Maritime provinces, when equalization payments are removed, are among those that spend the least and tax the least.

Marginal tax rates and the low-income trap

In the previous chapter, we mentioned that marginal tax rates discourage productive efforts. Table 6.7 ranks the provinces on their marginal tax rates in the first three income deciles and compares those provinces based on Statistics Canada's Low-Income Cut-Offs (1992 base). There appears to be a strong link. While such broad aggregates cannot "prove" that high tax rates are a cause of poverty, they raise a flag and may be one piece in the puzzle of why some people are "trapped" in low incomes.

Table 6.7: Marginal Tax Rates and Low Income Groups, 1998

	Percentage of families below LICO in the first 3 deciles		
	1	2	3
Newfoundland	99.2	31.7	24.5
Prince Edward Island	97.8	14.9	9.3
Nova Scotia	95.8	31.8	10.9
New Brunswick	100.0	38.6	10.7
Quebec	92.6	30.9	10.9
Ontario	89.6	20.2	8.9
Manitoba	97.2	34.8	12.8
Saskatchewan	98.6	21.4	13.5
Alberta	96.1	41.5	8.7
British Columbia	100.0	66.6	14.4
Canada	94.3	30.9	10.9

	Marginal tax rates (percent) faced when one moves:		
	1st – 2nd decile	2nd – 3rd decile	3rd – 4th decile
Newfoundland	4.0	30.2	27.0
Prince Edward Island	10.3	26.5	34.7
Nova Scotia	17.1	28.0	35.0
New Brunswick	9.9	25.7	38.3
Quebec	26.2	33.9	47.9
Ontario	29.2	35.9	41.1
Manitoba	12.7	39.7	33.1
Saskatchewan	8.7	49.6	30.3
Alberta	17.4	31.2	39.3
British Columbia	18.4	37.4	42.8
Canada	22.0	35.9	41.1

Source: The Fraser Institute, 1998.

Appendix

This appendix presents the tax calculations for two other family types, families and unattached individuals, the focus of chapters 3, 4, and 5, and families of four consisting of two parents and two children under the age of 18.

Table 6.8: Tax Rates for Families and Unattached Individuals, 1998 (%)

	Taxes to cash income	Taxes to total income before tax
Newfoundland	38.1	27.8
Prince Edward Island	41.7	28.9
Nova Scotia	42.0	29.2
New Brunswick	41.6	29.2
Quebec	47.4	33.0
Ontario	46.8	32.2
Manitoba	45.3	30.7
Saskatchewan	44.8	29.6
Alberta	44.2	30.1
British Columbia	49.0	33.3
Canada	46.4	31.9

Source: The Fraser Institute, 1998.

Table 6.9: Taxes of Families and Unattached Individuals, 1998 (dollars)

	Average cash income	Average total income before tax	Income tax	Sales tax	Amusement taxes*	Automobile taxes**	Payroll taxes***	Property tax	Import duties	Profits tax	Natural resource taxes	Other taxes	Total taxes
NF	41,510	56,925	6,222	2,953	1,402	734	2,183	672	119	916	76	553	15,830
PE	39,327	56,682	5,421	3,334	1,307	709	2,526	1,261	164	1,359	7	299	16,387
NS	42,819	61,613	6,537	3,283	1,497	706	2,806	1,351	157	1,487	16	161	18,000
NB	44,280	63,090	6,742	3,407	1,425	795	2,639	1,587	159	1,280	91	277	18,401
QC	43,708	62,722	7,732	3,513	1,235	694	4,416	1,307	179	1,372	43	223	20,714
ON	55,612	80,868	9,497	4,512	1,587	798	4,415	2,315	233	2,163	36	444	26,000
MB	48,308	71,335	7,148	3,488	1,744	632	3,165	2,045	193	2,323	53	1,101	21,891
SK	43,640	66,079	5,621	3,116	1,688	1,063	2,757	1,808	166	2,155	716	453	19,544
AB	54,074	79,338	9,395	1,815	1,951	656	4,126	1,723	217	2,229	1,031	755	23,898
BC	47,345	69,818	8,184	3,511	1,534	551	3,433	2,025	199	2,460	585	735	23,219
Canada	49,996	72,695	8,466	3,742	1,526	728	4,024	1,884	205	1,958	217	467	23,218

Source: The Fraser Institute, 1998.
*Amusement taxes include liquor, tobacco, amusement, and other excise taxes.
**Automobile taxes include Automobile, fuel, and motor vehicle license taxes.
***Payroll taxes include social security, pension, medical, and hospital taxes.

Table 6.10: Tax Rates for Families of Four (Parents and Two Children under 18 years), 1998 (percent)

	Taxes to cash income	Taxes to total income before tax
Newfoundland	41.2	29.7
Prince Edward Island	44.5	30.9
Nova Scotia	45.3	31.4
New Brunswick	44.4	31.0
Quebec	51.6	35.7
Ontario	47.9	33.4
Manitoba	45.3	31.6
Saskatchewan	45.7	30.6
Alberta	45.1	31.7
British Columbia	48.5	33.5
Canada	48.2	33.4
Source: The Fraser Institute, 1998.		

Table 6.11: Taxes of Families of Four (Parents and Two Children under 18 years), 1998 (dollars)

	Average cash income	Average total income before tax	Income tax	Sales tax	Amusement taxes*	Automobile taxes**	Payroll taxes***	Property tax	Import duties	Profits tax	Natural resource taxes	Other taxes	Total taxes
NF	52,965	73,488	9,189	4,317	2,050	1,073	3,371	301	175	410	143	797	21,825
PE	51,620	74,435	9,287	4,957	1,944	1,054	4,040	491	243	529	11	433	22,989
NS	62,297	89,826	12,322	5,511	2,513	1,186	4,927	569	264	626	30	269	28,217
NB	56,100	80,258	10,628	5,143	2,151	1,201	4,271	405	240	327	151	402	24,920
QC	59,580	86,164	12,994	5,430	1,908	1,073	6,858	871	276	913	76	344	30,744
ON	75,850	108,934	15,780	6,835	2,403	1,209	6,729	1,192	353	1,115	56	673	36,345
MB	61,136	87,692	11,411	5,093	2,546	922	5,029	350	281	398	78	1,594	27,701
SK	59,509	89,107	9,581	4,932	2,673	1,682	4,834	659	263	785	1,096	717	27,223
AB	75,275	107,151	16,211	2,822	3,034	1,020	6,211	623	338	806	1,709	1,161	33,935
BC	69,611	100,655	14,359	5,711	2,495	897	5,944	815	324	991	1,048	1,180	33,763
Canada	68,787	99,142	14,095	5,735	2,368	1,113	6,313	1,019	315	1,053	402	741	33,154

Source: The Fraser Institute, 1998.
*Amusement taxes include liquor, tobacco, amusement, and other excise taxes.
**Automobile taxes include Automobile, fuel, and motor vehicle license taxes.
***Payroll taxes include social security, pension, medical, and hospital taxes.

Chapter 7
Who Pays the Corporate Tax?

CORPORATIONS ARE A MAJOR SOURCE of revenue for federal and provincial governments. In 1997, they paid $29.1 billion in direct taxes, 9.0 percent of all federal and provincial government takings. These statements are factually correct but misleading. "Corporations" do not really bear the burden of these taxes—people do. This chapter explains which people end up paying these taxes. Even though we are well furnished with data on how much corporations pay and who owns them, determining who pays the corporate tax is not straightforward. A tax on corporations is a tax on capital. When the tax rises, capital will flee and this will affect what capital and labour earn and what consumers pay. Who truly ends up bearing the tax depends on all these affects. Our calculations suggest that the elderly bear the brunt of corporate taxation.

Background

A corporation is a group of people bound by contract to work together and to share the rewards of that work; in its simplest terms, it is a joint venture between capitalists and workers. This description is too rudimentary to be of much help in explaining why corporations exist and to what subtle incentives they respond, but it is all we need for the present discussion. Profits are what is left over after labour, interest on capital, and the cost of materials have been paid, and this residual amount can be thought of as going to the people who provided the capital for the business. Corporate tax falls on profits. This is why the corporate tax is a tax on capital.

There is often confusion over what the corporate tax rate is, because as well as having their profits taxed, corporations may receive special tax breaks that allow them to write off more than their true capital expenses. This means a corporation may pay a high statutory rate on its profits but a much lower actual rate because of its deductions.

Statutory rates on capital rose in the 1970s and 1980s but revenue from the corporate tax was unsteady because profits varied and deductions had increased, eroding the tax base. It is a general principle of taxation that, if one wants to raise a certain amount of revenue, one distorts people's choices less by imposing a low tax on a broad base than a high tax on a narrow base. By the mid-1980s, the base had become too narrow and this prompted the first stage of corporate tax reform. In the 1986 budget, the federal government started phasing out deductions such as the inventory allowance and the investment-tax credit and announced a leisurely pace at which it would reduce the statutory tax rate by 3 percent on average. However, tax reform in the United States lowered the corporate rate by 12 percent and this forced Canada to accelerate its own reforms, fearing that it would lose tax revenue to the United States because multinationals would report their revenue in the United States and their costs in Canada.

In 1987, many exemptions in the Canadian system were reduced and tax rates were decreased to 28 percent for large non-manufacturing firms, 23 percent for large manufacturing firms, and 12 percent for small firms. In 1998, the rates are 28 percent for large non-manufacturing firms, 21 percent for large manufacturing firms, and 12 percent for small firms. All provinces also levy corporate income tax, though at lower rates. Table 7.1 and the accompanying figure 7.1 show how federal and provincial corporate tax revenues have varied between 1967 and 1997.

Why is the corporate tax so popular?

The corporate tax has great political appeal. Ministers of finance argue convincingly that if a corporation makes profits it should pay taxes just as ordinary working people do. This argument is appealing but hides from Canadians the fact that, in the end, ordinary Canadians pay the corporate income tax. We can see this by asking what a corporation is: it is composed of machinery, contracts, office space, employees, shareholders, bondholders, and so on. These parts work together to make income for people and corporate tax is, therefore, a tax on *people*. The corporation itself cannot pay the tax because it is not the final destination of the income it generates. On the contrary, as the next sections show, taxes imposed on the corporation fan out to the general public by a path that is hard to trace. As J.B. Colbert said in 1665, "The art of taxation consists in so plucking the goose as to obtain the largest amount of feathers with the least possible

Table 7.1: Corporate Tax Collections, 1967 to 1997 ($millions 1997)

	Provincial	Federal	Total
1967	3,300	9,094	12,395
1969	3,934	11,538	15,472
1971	3,864	11,013	14,877
1973	5,920	15,019	20,939
1975	7,314	18,614	25,928
1977	6,099	14,893	20,992
1979	7,843	16,930	24,773
1981	7,132	19,144	26,276
1983	4,587	15,713	20,301
1985	5,935	17,291	23,226
1987	7,062	16,345	23,407
1989	8,164	15,394	23,558
1991	5,908	11,408	17,316
1993	5,136	10,593	15,729
1995	8,625	14,795	23,420
1997	11,081	18,011	29,092

Source: Statistics Canada, National Economic and Financial Accounts; calculations by the authors.

Figure 7.1: Revenue from Corporate Taxes, 1967–1997 ($billions 1997)

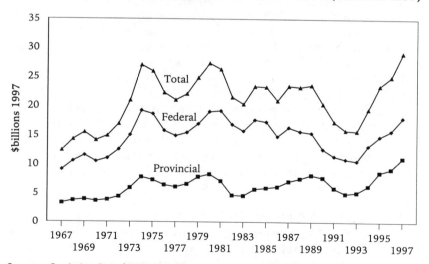

Sources: Statistics Canada, National Economic and Financial Accounts; calculations by the authors.

amount of hissing" (Mencken 1989: *s.v.* "Taxes") Corporate taxes cause less "hissing" than the more obvious taxes on sales or personal income. This is why politicians like the corporate tax.

Should it be so popular?

Who, in the end, pays the corporate tax? There are, of course, corporations owned by wealthy families and these families bear a portion of the tax. There are also many ordinary working people, however, who entrust their savings to mutual-fund managers. These managers invest this money in corporations and the income of those corporations flows back to these small investors. Approximately one-half of all Canadians now own shares, directly or indirectly, in the Canadian banks. Money set aside by employers for pensions is also invested in corporations. For example, OMERS, the Ontario Municipal Employees' Retirement System, is one of the largest stock owners and traders in Canada.

What is less obvious, but equally true, is that home-owners, farmers, cab drivers, and anyone who owns capital in the non-corporate sector of the economy also feels the impact of taxes on the corporate sector. How can this be? The reason is that capital is highly mobile. If the opportunities for making money in the corporate sector are reduced, investors will look for opportunities abroad or in the non-corporate sector at home. The non-corporate sector is largely made up of agriculture and real estate. As investors transfer their corporate capital to this sector, capital will become more abundant there and the returns to capital there will fall. For example, investors in high-technology stocks may find the corporate tax gives them too little return for the risks involved and they may decide to invest their money in apartment buildings. This will add to the number of rental apartments, increase the vacancy rate, and lower the margins of profit for landlords. Thus, the tax in the corporate high-technology sector can also affect the market for commercial real estate.

This is one of many possible examples that show why measuring who ultimately pays the corporate tax is a difficult task. There are other factors that add to the complexity of allocating the corporate tax burden: companies can pass the tax on in the form of higher prices or capital can simply leave the country, thereby making labour less productive and reducing wages.

Estimating the Canadian corporate tax

Since none of these assumptions can be dismissed out of hand, there is bound to be controversy over any estimate of who bears the corporate tax. This is why we provide several sets of calculations, each based on different, but plausible, assumptions. The main assumption we use in

Table 7.2: Decile Distribution of Profit Taxes (percent)

	Lower 3 deciles	Middle 4 deciles	Upper 3 deciles
1976	10.3	17.8	72.2
1981	9.1	24.0	66.9
1985	6.7	21.6	71.8
1990	5.8	24.5	69.7
1992	7.4	27.6	65.1
1994	7.0	27.4	65.7
1996	7.3	28.2	64.5
1998	8.0	30.1	62.0

Source: The Fraser Institute, 1998.

our calculations is that owners of capital in both corporate and non-corporate sectors bear the corporate tax but, for balance, we show what some of our results would look like if labour bore the entire tax or if it were shared between capital and labour.

Table 7.2 shows the breakdown of the corporate tax by lower-income, middle-income, and upper-income groups. As expected, the upper-income group bears most of this tax. Income deciles, however, do not tell us anything about the personal characteristics of taxpayers. A crucial question is how much of the tax various age groups pay. Table 7.3 and figure 7.2 show how much of all taxes that the government collects are paid by people of different age groups, and compares this to how much corporate tax each age group pays. Even though people above 65 pay little in overall taxes, they bear a disproportionate amount of the corporate tax.

These results are not surprising given our assumption that capital bears the tax. The elderly and the retired receive most of their income from capital sources such as retirement funds and rental property. For comparison, figure 7.3 shows how much different age groups would pay under the assumptions that (1) capital bears the entire tax; (2) capital and labour share the burden equally (*i.e.*, capital and labour bear the tax in proportion to their shares in national income); (3) labour bears the entire burden. As we can see, the results are very different depending on which assumptions one makes. How reasonable each assumption is depends on what we believe about the mobility of capital between corporate and non-corporate sectors and between Canada and the rest of the world. The more mobile capital is, the less of the burden of the tax it will bear. There is an active debate over the degree to which capital can pass the tax on to labour—a debate that we cannot resolve

Table 7.3: Total Tax and Corporate Tax Paid by Age Group, 1998

Age group	Corporate tax ($millions)	Share of corporate tax (percent)	Total tax ($millions)
16–23	104	0.4	2,463
24–31	614	2.4	23,846
32–39	1,885	7.2	52,576
40–47	2,930	11.2	68,164
48–55	3,803	14.6	57,390
56–63	4,165	16.0	33,780
64–71	5,597	21.4	22,435
72–79	4,498	17.2	16,129
80+	2,514	9.6	8,326

Source: The Fraser Institute, 1998.

here. The point to keep in mind is that it is people who pay the corporate tax. Under two of the three possible scenarios (capital bears all, capital and labour bear equally) the elderly pay significantly for a policy that is widely touted as a tax on the "rich."

The myth of the untaxed corporation

By now, it should be clear that the incidence of corporate tax is complex and that brash claims about it have to be examined cautiously. One particularly brash claim that often receives great attention from the Press is that some corporations in Canada are not paying their fair share of taxes. In particular, a labour-sponsored study claimed that 81,462 profitable corporations in Canada paid no taxes on profits of nearly $17.1 billion in 1994 and, as a result, have forced ordinary Canadians to shoulder a larger responsibility for paying the nation's taxes (British Columbia Federation of Labour 1997).

A study by the Ontario government's Fair Tax Commission shows a different picture. The Fair Tax Commission analyzed a special 1989 survey of 177,000 corporations in Ontario and reached the following conclusions.

- 54 percent of the profits that were not taxed were inter-corporate dividends or equity income earned by subsidiaries. That is, profits earned by one branch of the corporation were transferred, after they had been taxed, to another part of the corporation. Taxing these transfers of money would be like taxing a person for moving his wallet from one pocket to another.

Figure 7.2: Total Tax (left scale) and Corporate Tax (right scale)
by Age Group, 1998

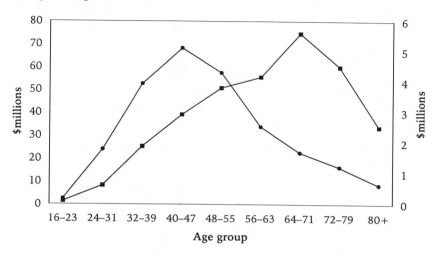

Source: The Fraser Institute, 1998.

Figure 7.3: Corporate Tax as a Percentage of Average Taxes Paid by Age
Group in 1998 under Three Incidence Assumptions

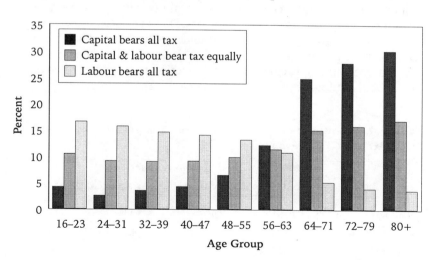

Sources: The Fraser Institute, 1998.

- 31 percent of profits were exempt either because they were used to replace depreciating equipment or because they were "paper gains," that is, assets transferred between members of the same corporate group without any economic gain or loss to the group.

- 11 percent of the profits not subject to tax were earned by firms that had lost money in the year before. The tax system takes the long view of profits and allows firms to carry their losses forward. If a corporation lost $1 million last year and earned $1 million this year, over two years it has not made any profit and so should not be taxed within this two-year cycle.

- 4 percent of profits were exempt from taxation because of the temporary small-business tax holiday.

In other words, in the view of the NDP government in Ontario at the time, the survey of corporations suggested that corporations were not unfairly avoiding taxes.

Those advocating new or increased corporate taxes and claiming that corporations are getting an "easy ride" avoid statistics that show that, in recent years, corporations pay significantly more than they did in the past. Table 7.1 shows that, when we remove the effects of inflation, corporations contribute significantly more to tax revenue now than they did in the 1960s. These critics focus on the proportion of corporate taxes in total taxes collected by government, which has fallen sharply since the 1950s and 1960s. This is deceptive because, as table 7.4 shows, while corporate tax revenues as a percent of total tax revenues have fallen by 46 percent, corporate taxes as a share of GDP have fallen by only 15 percent. Even though governments now get a smaller fraction of their revenues from corporations than they did in 1967, this has been caused by the unprecedented growth in personal taxation that we described earlier in the book and not by corporations cheating the tax system. Table 7.4

Table 7.4: Importance of Corporate and Personal Income Taxes in Government Tax Revenues

	Direct Taxes			
	As a percentage of total tax revenues		As a percentage of GDP	
Paid by	1961	1997	1961	1997
Corporations	16.6	9.0	4.0	3.4
Persons	22.9	37.5	5.5	14.1

Source: Statistics Canada, National Economic and Financial Accounts; calculations by the authors.

also shows that direct taxes on persons as a percent of total tax revenue increased by 64 percent from 1961 to 1997 and that direct taxes on persons as a percent of GDP increased by 156 percent.

Yet another perspective on the claim that corporations are not paying their fair share of tax comes from the work of economist Alan Douglas (Douglas 1990). He performed a subtle exercise to find the reasons that the corporate tax has declined as a share of total government revenue. He found that falling profits were the most significant reason for the decline: "if the profit rate for 1976 to 1985 had remained at its 1966–1975 average of 11.01 percent ... average [annual government] revenue would have been $11.31 billion instead of $7.55 billion. An extra $27.6 billion in corporate taxes would have been collected over the decade" (Douglas 1990: 70).

Table 7.5 supports this result; in almost every year shown, when corporate profits as a share of GDP increased, corporate taxes as a percent of total taxes increased. The converse is also true. Mr. Douglas found, in addition, that tax breaks, such as accelerated depreciation, reduced tax revenues much less than did declining profitability. Many of these tax breaks were eliminated in 1987 in any case. Until recently, corporations in Canada had known a long slide in profitability. Governments have not "taken it easy" on these corporations. Rather, it is simply that they have become a less lucrative and less reliable source of revenue than individual workers.

The fact that taxes upon corporations' profits depend upon the relative uncertainty of corporate profits is probably the main reason for the growing popularity of taxes upon corporate capital among the provinces. In 1987, four provinces imposed capital taxes on corporations and seven imposed capital taxes on banks. In 1997, only three provinces did not impose corporate capital taxes and all provinces taxed bank capital.

Table 7.5: Canadian Corporate Taxes

	GDP ($millions)	Corporate* profits before taxes ($millions)	Corporate* profits before tax as a percentage of GDP	Direct taxes from corporations* ($millions)*	Tax to profits (percent)	Corporate* tax as a percentage of total tax revenue
1961	41,253	4,498	10.9	1,649	36.7	16.6
1964	52,653	6,383	12.1	2,101	32.9	16.0
1967	69,834	7,697	11.0	2,396	31.1	12.4
1970	90,367	8,860	9.8	3,070	34.7	11.3
1973	129,196	16,888	13.1	5,079	30.1	12.8
1976	200,296	22,667	11.3	7,128	31.4	11.5
1979	280,309	38,822	13.8	10,038	25.9	12.3
1982	379,734	28,855	7.6	11,755	40.7	9.6
1985	485,139	54,168	11.2	15,563	28.7	10.1
1988	611,785	70,860	11.6	17,586	24.8	8.4
1991	683,239	37,254	5.5	15,015	40.3	6.0
1994	762,251	65,291	8.6	18,403	28.2	6.7
1995	799,129	76,872	9.6	22,201	28.9	7.7
1996	820,323	74,464	9.1	24,202	32.5	8.0
1997	856,134	86,534	10.1	29,088	33.6	9.0

Source: Statistics Canada; calculations by the authors.
*includes government business enterprises.

Chapter 8
Canada and the
Rest of the World

So FAR, we have concentrated our attention on how much tax Canadians pay and how those taxes have been changing. This is useful information if one wants to compare Canada today with Canada in the past. It is sufficient to concentrate on the tax burden within our own country provided one is fairly isolated from the rest of the world. However, new technology and falling trade barriers are weaving the economies of the world closer together than they have ever been before and stripping away any efforts at isolation. This means that, when we consider our taxes, we also have to look at the tax rates and levels in the countries with which we have close ties.

How do we compare?

The Canadian tax system is complex and no single number can summarize it. The same is true of comparisons between Canada and the rest of the world. Foreign tax systems are different and governments abroad provide their citizens with different levels of services. This means that comparing the total amount of taxes paid in Canada and in, say, Japan may tell us little about whether taxes are too high in one country relative to the other. For example, Canada may tax more than other countries but it may provide more and better public services. That is, the tax price of government activity may be lower here. This sort of subtlety does not mean, however, that international comparisons are meaningless. There are some numbers that can give us a broad feel for the differences between the systems.

Figure 8.1: International Comparison of Taxes Paid as a Percentage of GDP, 1996

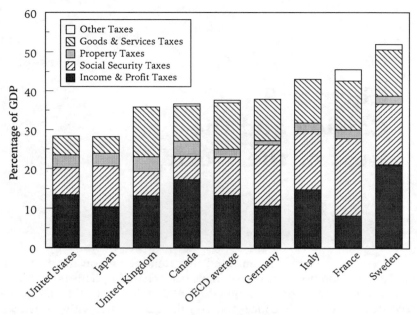

Source: OECD, Revenue Statistics, 1965–1997, 1998.

The level of taxes

Figure 8.1 shows the total amount of tax in Canada and other industrialized nations as a percentage of GDP in 1996. The vertical bar for each country is divided into five sections: income and profit taxes; social security taxes; property taxes; goods and services taxes; other taxes. Table 8.1 shows the numerical breakdown of the relative importance of each tax. The comparison shows that Canada falls in the middle among these nations. A closer look reveals that Canada has the highest income and profit taxes as a percentage of total taxes, the lowest social security taxes, and high property taxes. Some claim that these low social security taxes give Canada room to raise contribution rates but they miss certain facts.

- Canada's population is comparatively young so our social security taxes should be low. Japan has a relatively old population and social security taxes there are over one-third of the total tax bill.

Table 8.1: International Tax Comparisons, 1996

	Total tax as a percent of GDP	Taxes as a percent of total taxes				
		Income and Profits	Social Security	Property	Goods and Services	Other
United States	28.5	47.2	24.7	11.0	17.2	0.0
Japan	28.4	36.6	36.5	11.3	15.4	0.2
United Kingdom	36.0	36.8	17.3	10.6	35.2	0.1
Canada	36.8	47.3	16.3	10.4	24.9	1.1
OECD average	37.7	35.3	25.1	5.4	32.5	1.7
Germany	38.1	28.4	40.6	3.0	27.9	0.1
Italy	43.2	34.4	34.2	5.4	25.9	0.1
France	45.7	18.0	43.1	5.1	27.3	6.5
Sweden	52.0	41.0	29.8	3.8	22.8	2.6

Source: OECD, Revenue Statistics, 1965-1997, 1998.

- Canada Pension Plan contributions are already scheduled to increase from the 1997 rate of 6.0 percent to 9.9 percent in 2003.

- "Although payroll tax rates are low compared with other OECD countries, the same is not the case for total taxes payable on labour, including both income tax and social security contributions. The average effective rate on labour income in Canada is 29 percent, which is higher than all except the continental European OECD members." (Organisation for Economic Co-operation and Development 1997: 82).

- Canada's overall tax burden since 1965 has been rising rapidly. Table 8.2 shows that the percentage increase in our taxes as a share of GDP from 1965 to 1996 was 42.1 percent

- Canada's high debt represents a hidden tax that does not come out in this international comparison of visible taxes. Table 8.3 shows Canada's government debt as a fraction of GDP and compares it to other industrialized countries. Only Italy among the G-7 countries has a ratio of debt to GDP higher than that of Canada. Among the 18 OECD countries that report comparable debt statistics, Canada has the third highest ratio, ahead of only Italy and Belgium (Alexander and Emes 1998).

Table 8.2: Percentage Change in Taxes From 1965 to 1996

	Total change (Percentage)	Change by tax type (Percentage)			
		Profit and Income	Social Security	Property	Goods and Services
United States	17.3	15.4	118.8	-20.5	–10.9
Japan	55.2	30.0	160.0	113.3	–8.3
United Kingdom	18.4	16.8	31.9	–13.6	25.7
Canada	42.1	74.0	328.6	2.7	–13.3
OECD average	45.0	47.3	104.2	0.0	23.7
Germany	20.6	0.9	82.4	–38.9	1.9
Italy	69.4	223.9	70.1	27.8	10.9
France	32.5	49.1	66.9	53.3	–5.3
Sweden	48.6	10.9	269.0	233.3	8.3

Source: OECD, Revenue Statistics, 1965–1997, 1998.

Why bother comparing?

Comparing taxes is interesting because it indicates how well a country can compete in the international marketplace. Taxes raise the costs facing a business and, if there is no offsetting movement in the exchange rate, they may cripple its ability to undersell foreign competitors who come from countries with lower tax burdens. We must be careful before jumping to conclusions, however, because in return for paying taxes we receive government services that help us to be productive. Infrastructures such as roads, schools, and legal and penal systems that work as they should are all vital aids to success in facing the challenge of foreign competition. This means that we have to ask whether a rising trend in Canadian and other taxes represents heavier investments in these productive infrastructures. It is imaginable that a higher tax burden does not represent a competitive disadvantage provided those taxes are being spent productively by government.

Table 8.3: Net Government Debt as a Percentage of GDP, 1998 (estimate)

Sweden	19.7	United States	45.5
Japan	26.9	Germany	50.2
United Kingdom	42.7	Canada	60.0
France	44.8	Italy	106.2

Source: OECD, *OECD Economic Outlook*, 63, June 1998.

The evidence from 1966 to 1995 in table 8.4 shows that as a fraction of government budgets, these vital infrastructures are falling in Canada. A greater fraction of our tax dollar is going to finance interest payments on the debt and social security programs. These expenditures make up roughly two-thirds of government budgets. A similar picture emerges for many of the foreign countries with which we have been comparing Canada in this chapter. Two economists from the International Monetary Fund recently released a study on the growth of government spending in 17 industrialized countries, including Canada (Tanzi and Schuknecht 1995). The study shows that between 1960 and 1994

- average government spending increased from 27.9 to 47.2 percent of GDP;

- average spending on interest payments increased from 1.9 to 4.3 percent of GDP;

- average spending on subsidies and transfers increased from 8.3 to 23.0 percent of GDP;

- these increased spending levels did not improve performance on basic social indicators.

These results imply that industrialized less developed countries and more developed countries with a small government sector could have an advantage over us if they have a smaller tax burden and still manage to attain the same basic social results.

Canada and the United States

The United States buys about 81 percent of Canada's exports. The proximity of the United States and the increasing flow of goods and services over our border because of NAFTA means that it is the tax system of the United States with which we ought particularly to compare our tax system. According to economist Brian Bethune, taxes are about 27 percent higher in Canada than in the United States (Bethune 1993).

The OECD, in its recent country survey for Canada (Organisation for Economic Cooperation and Development 1997), noted the following.

- Relative to the United States, personal income tax rates are quite high, especially for those with high incomes subject to federal and provincial surtaxes. For example, according to calculations by the OECD Secretariat, the marginal tax rate for a person earning twice the average production wage is 48 percent in Canada, compared with 43 percent in the United States and 47 percent in all OECD

Table 8.4: Composition of Total Government Spending, 1966 and 1995

	1965/66		1994/95		Change in percent of total from 1965/66 to 1994/95
	$millions	Percent of total	$millions	Percent of total	
General services	966	5.6	18,237	5.1	-0.5
Protection of persons & property	2,268	13.2	24,477	6.8	-6.3
Transportation & communication	2,149	12.5	15,689	4.4	-8.1
Health	1,678	9.8	47,100	13.2	3.4
Social services	3,112	18.1	85,783	24.0	5.9
Education	2,982	17.3	43,920	12.3	-5.0
Resource conservation and industrial development	870	5.1	14,119	3.9	-1.1
Environment	435	2.5	8,040	2.2	-0.3
Recreation & Culture	257	1.5	7,215	2.0	0.5
Labour, Employment and Immigration	51	0.3	3,311	0.9	0.6
Housing	23	0.1	3,828	1.1	0.9
Foreign affairs and international assistance	159	0.9	4,934	1.4	0.5
Regional planning & development	80	0.5	1,615	0.5	-0.0
Research establishments	68	0.4	2,073	0.6	0.2
Transfers to own enterprises	270	1.6	5,113	1.4	-0.1
Debt charges	1,718	10.0	71,325	19.9	10.0
Other Expenditures	122	0.7	791	0.2	-0.5
Total expenditures	17,207	100.0	357,568	100.0	0.0

Source: Statistics Canada, Public Finance Historical Data, 1965/66-1991/92, catalogue 68-512; Public Sector Finance, 1995/96, catalogue 68-212; calculations by the authors.

countries. Similar differentials exist for average tax rates. This could make it more difficult to attract and retain highly skilled persons, who are likely to be the most mobile internationally.

- The disincentive imposed on investment by corporate taxes and other taxes on business income tends to be relatively high for large firms. A recent study (Chen and McKenzie 1996) found that the marginal effective tax rate on investment in manufacturing was higher in Canada than in all the countries studied except Germany and Japan. Similar patterns prevailed for services, with the differential between Canada and the United States, in particular, being even larger.

Compared to our main trading partner, the United States, our tax rates and levels are high. Compared to other industrialized countries, our debt burden and resultant interest costs as a share of total government spending are high. These issues deserve serious attention, especially in the face of falling trade barriers and increasing globalization.

Appendix 1
Calculate How Much Tax
You Really Pay

THIS APPENDIX is a simple tool that will help you discover how much tax you really pay. It takes a bit of work but arriving at the final result requires only a few minutes and some calculator strokes. The tables that follow show what are known as "regression estimates" of the tax system. We have tried to relate how much tax families pay to characteristics such as age and sex of the head of the family, size of the family, and different sources of income. The formulas that we have developed will give you an approximate idea of your total taxes. If you want a quick but less precise calculation, use the first set of tables. Here is how you would proceed if you were a 45-year-old male head of a family of four living in Newfoundland, with a family income of $50,000.

Sample quick table

Characteristics	Coefficient (1)	You (2)	Multiple (1) × (2)
Family size	–2,793	× 4	= –11,172
Age of head	–172	× 45	= –7,740
Sex of head (0 if male, 1 if female)	1,296	× 1	= 1,296
Family income	0.75	× 50,000	= 37,500
Adjustment factor	2,847		= 2,847
Total			= 21,435

The column under "Coefficient," which we provide, is used to multiply the column "You," which you complete with your personal characteristics. This gives a column called "Multiple," which is then summed (including what we provide as an adjustment factor). The sum is an estimate of your family's total tax bill. We provide these simple tables for all ten provinces. There are also a set of more detailed tables for the ten provinces. The detailed tables enable you to calculate a more precise estimate of your family's total tax bill; we recommend that you use these. Simply follow the procedure outlined above. Here is how the same hypothetical individual described above would proceed.

We assume that the family's income, $50,000, is made up as follows: $39,950 in salaries and wages; $2,900 in self-employment income; $2,500 in investment income; $4,650 in personal transfers from the government.

Sample detailed table

Characteristics	Coefficient (1)	You (2)	Multiple (1) × (2)
Family size	−772	× 4	= −3,088
Age of head	−24	× 45	= −1,080
Sex of head (0 if male, 1 if female)	330	× 1	= 0
Income from salaries & wages	0.62	× 39,950	= 24,569
Income from self-employment	0.45	× 2,900	= 1,302
Income from investment	1.03	× 2,500	= 2,567
Income from farming	0.13	× 0	= 0
Income from pensions	1.20	× 0	= 0
Income from government transfers	0.11	× 4,650	= 530
Square of salaries & wages	5.3×10^{-7}	× $(39,950)^2$	= 846
Square of self-employed income	4.9×10^{-7}	× $(2,900)^2$	= 4
Square of investment income	-1.8×10^{-7}	× $(2,500)^2$	= −1
Square of farm income	2.0×10^{-5}	× $(0)^2$	= 0
Square of pension income	7.1×10^{-6}	× $(0)^2$	= 0
Square of transfer income	5.6×10^{-7}	× $(4,650)^2$	= −12
Adjustment factor	397		= 397
Total			= 26,034

Table A.1: Newfoundland

Quick table

Characteristics	Coefficient (1)	You (2)	Multiple (1) × (2)
Family size	-2,793	× _____	= _____
Age of head	-172	× _____	= _____
Sex of head (0 if male, 1 if female)	1,296	× _____	= _____
Family income	0.75	× _____	= _____
Adjustment factor	2,847		= 2,847
Total			=

Detailed table

Characteristics	Coefficient (1)	You (2)	Multiple (1) × (2)
Family size	-722	× _____	= _____
Age of head	-24	× _____	= _____
Sex of head (0 if male, 1 if female)	330	× _____	= _____
Income from salaries & wages	0.62	× _____	= _____
Income from self-employment	0.45	× _____	= _____
Income from investment	1.03	× _____	= _____
Income from farming	0.13	× _____	= _____
Income from pensions	1.19	× _____	= _____
Income from government transfers	0.11	× _____	= _____
Square of salaries & wages	5.3×10^{-7}	× (_____)^2	= _____
Square of self-employed income	4.9×10^{-7}	× (_____)^2	= _____
Square of investment income	-1.8×10^{-7}	× (_____)^2	= _____
Square of farm income	2.0×10^{-5}	× (_____)^2	= _____
Square of pension income	7.1×10^{-6}	× (_____)^2	= _____
Square of transfer income	5.6×10^{-7}	× (_____)^2	= _____
Adjustment factor	1,430		= 1,430
Total			=

Table A.2: Prince Edward Island

Quick table

Characteristics	Coefficient (1)	You (2)	Multiple (1) × (2)
Family size	−1,020	× _____	= _____
Age of head	−55	× _____	= _____
Sex of head (0 if male, 1 if female)	1,105	× _____	= _____
Family income	0.52	× _____	= _____
Adjustment factor	185		= 185
Total			=

Detailed table

Characteristics	Coefficient (1)	You (2)	Multiple (1) × (2)
Family size	−571	× _____	= _____
Age of head	−12	× _____	= _____
Sex of head (0 if male, 1 if female)	140	× _____	= _____
Income from salaries & wages	0.54	× _____	= _____
Income from self-employment	0.27	× _____	= _____
Income from investment	1.41	× _____	= _____
Income from farming	0.28	× _____	= _____
Income from pensions	1.41	× _____	= _____
Income from government transfers	0.13	× _____	= _____
Square of salaries & wages	1.7×10^{-7}	× (_____)^2	= _____
Square of self-employed income	2.4×10^{-7}	× (_____)^2	= _____
Square of investment income	-2.6×10^{-6}	× (_____)^2	= _____
Square of farm income	4.4×10^{-7}	× (_____)^2	= _____
Square of pension income	-2.5×10^{-6}	× (_____)^2	= _____
Square of transfer income	-9.2×10^{-7}	× (_____)^2	= _____
Adjustment factor	−443		= −443
Total			=

Table A.3: Nova Scotia

Quick table

Characteristics	Coefficient (1)	You (2)	Multiple (1) × (2)
Family size	−2,394	× _____	= _____
Age of head	−47	× _____	= _____
Sex of head (0 if male, 1 if female)	861	× _____	= _____
Family income	0.66	× _____	= _____
Adjustment factor	−1,701		= −1,701
Total			=

Detailed table

Characteristics:	Coefficient (1)	You (2)	Multiple (1) × (2)
Family size	−836	× _____	= _____
Age of head	−14	× _____	= _____
Sex of head (0 if male, 1 if female)	307	× _____	= _____
Income from salaries & wages	0.55	× _____	= _____
Income from self-employment	0.39	× _____	= _____
Income from investment	1.03	× _____	= _____
Income from farming	−.01	× _____	= _____
Income from pensions	1.11	× _____	= _____
Income from government transfers	0.22	× _____	= _____
Square of salaries & wages	1.8×10^{-7}	× (_____)^2	= _____
Square of self-employed income	7.3×10^{-8}	× (_____)^2	= _____
Square of investment income	6.1×10^{-8}	× (_____)^2	= _____
Square of farm income	1.1×10^{-6}	× (_____)^2	= _____
Square of pension income	4.7×10^{-7}	× (_____)^2	= _____
Square of transfer income	-2.4×10^{-6}	× (_____)^2	= _____
Adjustment factor	−1,152		= 1,152
Total			=

Table A.4: New Brunswick

Quick table

Characteristics	Coefficient (1)	You (2)	Multiple (1) × (2)
Family size	-2,736	× _____	= _____
Age of head	-97	× _____	= _____
Sex of head (0 if male, 1 if female)	1,047	× _____	= _____
Family income	0.71	× _____	= _____
Adjustment factor	–337		= –337
Total			=

Detailed table

Characteristics	Coefficient (1)	You (2)	Multiple (1) × (2)
Family size	–786	× _____	= _____
Age of head	–28	× _____	= _____
Sex of head (0 if male, 1 if female)	27	× _____	= _____
Income from salaries & wages	0.54	× _____	= _____
Income from self-employment	0.47	× _____	= _____
Income from investment	1.28	× _____	= _____
Income from farming	0.21	× _____	= _____
Income from pensions	1.07	× _____	= _____
Income from government transfers	0.21	× _____	= _____
Square of salaries & wages	3.0×10^{-7}	× (_____)^2	= _____
Square of self-employed income	2.53×10^{-7}	× (_____)^2	= _____
Square of investment income	-5.83×10^{-7}	× (_____)^2	= _____
Square of farm income	2.1×10^{-6}	× (_____)^2	= _____
Square of pension income	2.6×10^{-6}	× (_____)^2	= _____
Square of transfer income	-2.5×10^{-6}	× (_____)^2	= _____
Adjustment factor	187		= 187
Total			=

Table A.5: Quebec

Quick table

Characteristics	Coefficient (1)	You (2)	Multiple (1) × (2)
Family size	−2,610	× _____	= _____
Age of head	−53	× _____	= _____
Sex of head (0 if male, 1 if female	−94	× _____	= _____
Family income	0.72	× _____	= _____
Adjustment factor	−862		= −862
Total			= _____

Detailed table

Characteristics	Coefficient (1)	You (2)	Multiple (1) × (2)
Family size	−1,385	× _____	= _____
Age of head	−23	× _____	= _____
Sex of head (0 if male, 1 if female)	247	× _____	= _____
Income from salaries & wages	0.63	× _____	= _____
Income from self-employment	0.49	× _____	= _____
Income from investment	1.44	× _____	= _____
Income from farming	0.40	× _____	= _____
Income from pensions	1.32	× _____	= _____
Income from government transfers	0.25	× _____	= _____
Square of salaries & wages	1.6×10^{-7}	× (_____)^2	= _____
Square of self-employed income	6.2×10^{-8}	× (_____)^2	= _____
Square of investment income	-6.7×10^{-7}	× (_____)^2	= _____
Square of farm income	-1.9×10^{-7}	× (_____)^2	= _____
Square of pension income	4.5×10^{-6}	× (_____)^2	= _____
Square of transfer income	-2.0×10^{-6}	× (_____)^2	= _____
Adjustment factor	418		= 418
Total			= _____

Table A.6: Ontario

Quick table

Characteristics	Coefficient (1)	You (2)	Multiple (1) × (2)
Family size	−3,107	× _____	= _____
Age of head	37	× _____	= _____
Sex of head (0 if male, 1 if female)	764	× _____	= _____
Family income	0.73	× _____	= _____
Adjustment factor	−7,696		= −7,696
Total			= _____

Detailed table

Characteristics	Coefficient (1)	You (2)	Multiple (1) × (2)
Family size	−1,799	× _____	= _____
Age of head	−57	× _____	= _____
Sex of head (0 if male, 1 if female)	633	× _____	= _____
Income from salaries & wages	0.61	× _____	= _____
Income from self-employment	0.56	× _____	= _____
Income from investment	1.35	× _____	= _____
Income from farming	−0.23	× _____	= _____
Income from pensions	1.48	× _____	= _____
Income from government transfers	0.60	× _____	= _____
Square of salaries & wages	5.77×10^{-7}	× (_____)^2	= _____
Square of self-employed income	-8.9×10^{-9}	× (_____)^2	= _____
Square of investment income	-1.2×10^{-7}	× (_____)^2	= _____
Square of farm income	7.4×10^{-6}	× (_____)^2	= _____
Square of pension income	2.1×10^{-7}	× (_____)^2	= _____
Square of transfer income	-9.11×10^{-6}	× (_____)^2	= _____
Adjustment factor	−2,171		= −2,171
Total			= _____

Table A.7: Manitoba

Quick table

Characteristics	Coefficient (1)	You (2)	Multiple (1) × (2)
Family size	−2,869	× _____	= _____
Age of head	-83	× _____	= _____
Sex of head (0 if male, 1 if female)	769	× _____	= _____
Family income	0.75	× _____	= _____
Adjustment factor	−2,009		= −2,009
Total			= _____

Detailed table

Characteristics	Coefficient (1)	You (2)	Multiple (1) × (2)
Family size	−1,057	× _____	= _____
Age of head	−26	× _____	= _____
Sex of head (0 if male, 1 if female)	481	× _____	= _____
Income from salaries & wages	0.56	× _____	= _____
Income from self-employment	0.61	× _____	= _____
Income from investment	1.42	× _____	= _____
Income from farming	0.70	× _____	= _____
Income from pensions	1.25	× _____	= _____
Income from government transfers	0.22	× _____	= _____
Square of salaries & wages	1.4×10^{-7}	× (_____)^2	= _____
Square of self-employed income	8.7×10^{-8}	× (_____)^2	= _____
Square of investment income	-6.82×10^{-7}	× (_____)^2	= _____
Square of farm income	7.8×10^{-7}	× (_____)^2	= _____
Square of pension income	2.6×10^{-6}	× (_____)^2	= _____
Square of transfer income	-2.36×10^{-6}	× (_____)^2	= _____
Adjustment factor	−868		= −868
Total			= _____

Table A.8: Saskatchewan

Quick table

Characteristics	Coefficient (1)	You (2)	Multiple (1) × (2)
Family size	−1,849	× _____	= _____
Age of head	−17	× _____	= _____
Sex of head (0 if male, 1 if female)	−107	× _____	= _____
Family income	0.67	× _____	= _____
Adjustment factor	−3,272		= −3,272
Total			=

Detailed table

Characteristics	Coefficient (1)	You (2)	Multiple (1) × (2)
Family size	−697	× _____	= _____
Age of head	−21	× _____	= _____
Sex of head (0 if male, 1 if female)	267	× _____	= _____
Income from salaries & wages	0.51	× _____	= _____
Income from self-employment	0.50	× _____	= _____
Income from investment	1.57	× _____	= _____
Income from farming	1.08	× _____	= _____
Income from pensions	1.72	× _____	= _____
Income from government transfers	0.23	× _____	= _____
Square of salaries & wages	9.7×10^{-8}	× (_____)^2	= _____
Square of self-employed income	1.6×10^{-7}	× (_____)^2	= _____
Square of investment income	-6.4×10^{-7}	× (_____)^2	= _____
Square of farm income	7.1×10^{-6}	× (_____)^2	= _____
Square of pension income	6.1×10^{-6}	× (_____)^2	= _____
Square of transfer income	-3.0×10^{-6}	× (_____)^2	= _____
Adjustment factor	−854		= −854
Total			=

Table A.9: Alberta

Quick table

Characteristics	Coefficient (1)	You (2)	Multiple (1) × (2)
Family size	−2,221	× _____	= _____
Age of head	−15	× _____	= _____
Sex of head (0 if male, 1 if female)	787	× _____	= _____
Family income	0.66	× _____	= _____
Adjustment factor	−5,004		= −5,004
Total			=

Detailed table

Characteristics	Coefficient (1)	You (2)	Multiple (1) × (2)
Family size	−620	× _____	= _____
Age of head	−19	× _____	= _____
Sex of head (0 if male, 1 if female)	64	× _____	= _____
Income from salaries & wages	0.49	× _____	= _____
Income from self-employment	0.45	× _____	= _____
Income from investment	1.04	× _____	= _____
Income from farming	0.56	× _____	= _____
Income from pensions	1.21	× _____	= _____
Income from government transfers	0.24	× _____	= _____
Square of salaries & wages	1.1×10^{-7}	× (_____)^2	= _____
Square of self-employed income	9.3×10^{-8}	× (_____)^2	= _____
Square of investment income	3.6×10^{-8}	× (_____)^2	= _____
Square of farm income	-9.2×10^{-8}	× (_____)^2	= _____
Square of pension income	2.1×10^{-6}	× (_____)^2	= _____
Square of transfer income	-2.9×10^{-6}	× (_____)^2	= _____
Adjustment factor	−1,064		= −1,064
Total			=

Table A.10: British Columbia

Quick table

	Coefficient	You	Multiple
Characteristics	(1)	(2)	(1) × (2)
Family size	−838	× _____	= _____
Age of head	31	× _____	= _____
Sex of head (0 if male, 1 if female)	243	× _____	= _____
Family income	0.64	× _____	= _____
Adjustment factor	−6,026		= −6,026
Total			=

Detailed table

	Coefficient	You	Multiple
Characteristics	(1)	(2)	(1) × (2)
Family size	−488	× _____	= _____
Age of head	−7	× _____	= _____
Sex of head (0 if male, 1 if female)	−18	× _____	= _____
Income from salaries & wages	0.54	× _____	= _____
Income from self-employment	0.38	× _____	= _____
Income from investment	1.2	× _____	= _____
Income from farming	0.01	× _____	= _____
Income from pensions	1.34	× _____	= _____
Income from government transfers	0.19	× _____	= _____
Square of salaries & wages	1.5×10^{-7}	× (_____$)^2$	= _____
Square of self-employed income	5.0×10^{-7}	× (_____$)^2$	= _____
Square of investment income	-5.0×10^{-8}	× (_____$)^2$	= _____
Square of farm income	-3.7×10^{-6}	× (_____$)^2$	= _____
Square of pension income	1.0×10^{-5}	× (_____$)^2$	= _____
Square of transfer income	-2.1×10^{-6}	× (_____$)^2$	= _____
Adjustment factor	−1,028		= −1,028
Total			=

Glossary of Principal Terms, Measures, and Concepts

Indices

(1) **Index** is a method of measuring the percentage changes from a base year of a certain item, such as the price, volume, or value of food or the dollar amount of taxes. In order to construct an index, the price, volume, or value of the particular item being indexed in each year is divided by the price, volume, or value of the item in the base year; it is then multiplied by 100. An index has a value of 100 in the base year. In this book, the base year is 1961.

(2) **Consumer Price Index** measures the percentage change from a base year in the cost of purchasing a constant "basket" of goods and services representing the purchases by a particular population group in a specified time period. The *Consumer Price Index* (CPI) reflects price movements of some 300 items. The CPI is calculated monthly by *Statistics Canada* (see below).

(3) **Consumer Tax Index** measures the percentage change from a base year in the average Canadian family's tax bill. The Consumer Tax Index (CTI) is composed of federal, provincial, and municipal taxes. The CTI, calculated by The Fraser Institute, was introduced by the Institute for the first time in the first edition of *Tax Facts*, which was entitled *How Much Tax Do You Really Pay?*

(4) *Balanced Budget Tax Index* is the same as the *Consumer Tax Index* except that also included in the calculation is the amount of tax that would have to be raised if governments did not issue debt and were, in fact, balancing their budgets. This index was introduced by The Fraser Institute for the first time in the second edition of the *Tax Facts* series, *Tax Facts: The Canadian Consumer Tax Index and You.*

Statistical terms

(5) *Average Canadian Family* represents a family that had average income in a particular year. The averages were constructed from Statistics Canada's expenditure and income surveys, details of which appear in the bibliography.

(6) *Family* refers to a group of persons dependent upon a common or pooled income for their major expenditure items and living in the same dwelling. The term also applies to a financially independent unattached individual living alone.

(7) *Family Expenditure Survey* refers to the Statistics Canada surveys that show patterns of family expenditure for Canada by selected characteristics such as urban or rural area, family type, life cycle, income, age of head, tenure, occupation of head, education of head, country of origin and immigrant arrival year.

(8) *Shelter expenditure* is included as one of the selected expenditure items in this book. It refers to expenditures on rented or owned living quarters or repairs to these quarters; on mortgage interest and on other housing, such as vacation homes, lodging at university or at remote work locations. It also includes expenditures on water and heating fuel.

(9) *Statistics Canada* is Canada's official statistical agency, often referred to as "StatsCan." Statistics Canada provided much of the published and unpublished data for this book. For a detailed listing of these sources, see *Government sources*, in References.

(10) *Survey of Consumer Finances* refers to the survey from Statistics Canada that gives details of the incomes and characteristics of families. Information is given on the incomes (from, *e.g.*, salaries, wages, and pensions) of the head of family and of the spouse, residence (*e.g.*, province, rural or urban), personal characteristics (*e.g.* family size,

age and educational level of head and spouse), and labour-related characteristics (*e.g.* occupation, employment status).

Income concepts

(11) *Cash income* is the income that a family would report when completing a government survey, such as the Family Expenditure Survey, the Survey of Consumer Finances, or the Census form. It includes income that one receives regularly, such as salary or wage income (before tax) and payments from government such as old age security, unemployment insurance and family allowances. Families generally under-report their income so cash income estimates used in this study are "bumped up" using a Statistics Canada adjustment to include income that is often omitted when a family reports its income. Income which is often excluded is bond or bank interest and dividend income.

(12) *Deciles* are a way of categorizing families. All families were arranged according to total income before tax, from lowest income to highest, and then divided into ten groups, i.e. the first decile contains the 10 percent of families with the lowest incomes, the second decile contains the 10 percent of families with the second lowest incomes, etc.

(13) *Hidden income* is income that a family receives but probably does not consider to be a part of its income. Hidden income is largely made up of employer contributions to pension plans, medical premiums, and insurance plans. Another example is imputed non-farm rent. (For a more complete discussion of imputed non-farm rent see The Fraser Institute publication *Rent Control—A Popular Paradox*, p. 33).

(14) *Income from government* is income that a family receives as payment from the government, whereas taxes are payments to the government. Therefore, income from the government can be considered a "negative tax." It is often referred to as a transfer payment. It includes such items as family allowance payments, old age security payments, veterans' grants, etc.

(15) *Total income before tax* is the term used in this book to designate the amount of income the family would have received before paying tax. It is composed of cash income which includes income from government (transfer payments), and hidden income.

(16) *Transfer payments*, see *Income from government* above.

About taxes

(17) *Balanced budget tax rate* is the tax rate that Canadians would face if governments had to balance their budgets and finance all expenditures from current tax revenue instead of issuing debt.

(18) *Corporate profits tax* is the tax paid on the profits of a corporation. This is also referred to as the corporate income tax.

(19) *Deferred taxation* the debt incurred by the various levels of government to finance the expenditures that cannot be met by current tax revenue is, in effect, deferred taxation because the debts and interest on them must ultimately be paid out of future tax revenue.

(20) *Direct taxes* are taxes which are paid directly by the family. Examples of direct taxes are the personal income tax and provincial retail sales taxes. They are often referred to as explicit taxes.

(21) *Hidden taxes* are taxes that are concealed in the price of articles that one buys. Hidden taxes are also referred to as implicit taxes. The most well-known form of the hidden tax is the indirect tax. Examples of hidden taxes are the tobacco, fuel, and alcohol taxes and import duties.

(22) *Negative tax,* see *Income from government* above.

(23) *Progressive, proportional and regressive taxation* are terms that refer to the proportionality of taxes on income. A tax is called proportional if it takes the same fraction of income from low income people as it does from high income people. (Unemployment Insurance payments and Canada Pension payments up to the maximum earnings level are examples of proportional taxes). A progressive tax is one that takes a greater proportion of income from high income people than from those with low incomes (income tax, for example). A regressive tax is one that takes a greater proportion of income from low income people than it does from high income people (sales tax, for example).

(24) *Social security taxes* are composed of both federal and provincial taxes. The federal category includes employer and employee contributions to public service pensions and to Unemployment Insurance. Provincial social security taxes include employer and employee contributions to public service pensions, employer and employee contributions to Workers' Compensation and Industrial Employees' Vacations. Also in-

cluded in this category as taxes are payments to the Canada and Quebec Pension Plans and medical and hospital insurance premiums.

(25) *Tax burden* is the means of determining who ultimately pays tax and is synonymous with the term "tax incidence." Tax burden is measured by the decline in real purchasing power that results from the imposition of a tax.

(26) *Taxation powers under the Constitution of Canada.* The general scheme of taxation in the British North America Act can be summarized in this way:

1. the federal government is given an unlimited power to tax.

2. the provinces are also given what amounts to an unlimited power to tax "within the province;" that is to say, an unlimited power to tax persons within their jurisdiction and to impose taxes in respect to property located and income earned within the province. But their taxing powers are framed in such a way as to preclude them from imposing taxes that would have the effect of creating barriers to interprovincial trade and, generally, from taxing persons and property outside the province.

References

Alexander, Jared, and Joel Emes (1998). *Canadian Government Debt: A Guide to the Indebtedness of Canada and the Provinces.* Vancouver, BC: The Fraser Institute.

Bethune, Brian A. (1993). The Competitiveness of the Canadian Tax System. *Canadian Tax Journal* 41, 6: 1119–27

Bird, Richard M. (1970). *Growth of Government Spending in Canada.* Canadian Tax Foundation (July).

British Columbia Federation of Labour (1997). *Corporate Tax Freedom Day.* Press release (January 28).

Browning, Edgar K. (1978). The Burden of Taxation. *Journal of Political Economy* 86, 4 (August): 649–71.

Browning, Edgar K., and William R. Johnson (1979). *The Distribution of the Tax Burden.* American Enterprise Institute.

Burrows, Marie. *Fiscal Positions of the Provinces: The 1983 Budgets.* Conference Board of Canada; Aeric Inc.

Campbell, Harry F. 1975). An Input-Output Analysis of the Commodity Structure of Indirect Taxes in Canada. *Canadian Journal of Economics* (August): 433.

Canadian Bankers Association (1998). *Canadian Bank Facts, 1997/98.*

Canadian Institute of Actuaries (1995). *Troubled Tomorrows: The Report of the Institute of Actuaries' Task Force on Retirement Savings* (January).

Canadian Tax Foundation (various issues). *Finances of the Nation: A Review of Expenditures and Revenues of the Federal, Provincial, and Local Governments of Canada, 1995.*

——— (various issues). *The National Finances: An Analysis of the Revenues and Expenditures of the Government of Canada.*

——— (various issues). *Provincial and Municipal Finances.*

Chen, Duanjie, and Kenneth J. McKenzie (1996). *The Impact of Taxation on Capital Markets: An International Comparison of Effective Tax Rates on Capital.* Prepared for "Capital Market Issues," a conference sponsored by Industry Canada.

Conference Board of Canada (1996). *Provincial Outlook* 11, 2 (Spring).

Davies, James, France St.-Hilaire, and John Whalley (1984). Some Calculations of Lifetime Tax Incidence. *American Economic Review* 74, 4 (September): 633–49.

Dodge, David A. (1975). Impact of Tax, Transfer and Expenditure Policies of Government on the Distribution of Personal Incomes in Canada. *Review of Income and Wealth* 21, 1 (March): 1–52.

Douglas, Alan V. (1990). Changes in Corporate Tax Revenue. *Canadian Tax Journal* 38, 1 (Jan./Feb): 66–81.

Gillespie, W. Irwin (1966). *Incidence of Taxes and Public Expenditures in the Canadian Economy*. Studies of the Royal Commission on Taxation 2.

——— (1978). *In Search of Robin Hood*. Toronto, ON: C.D. Howe Research Institute.

Goffman, Irving J. (1972). *The Burden of Canadian Taxation*. Tax Paper 29 (July). Canadian Tax Foundation.

Horry, Isabella D., and Michael A. Walker (1994). *Government Spending Facts 2*. Vancouver, BC: The Fraser Institute.

La Forest, G. V. (1981). *The Allocation of Taxing Power under the Canadian Constitution*. Canadian Tax Foundation.

Lewis, Perrin (1978). The Tangled Tale of Taxes and Transfers. In Michael Walker (ed.), *Canadian Confederation at the Crossroads: The Search for a Federal-Provincial Balance* (Vancouver, BC: The Fraser Institute): 39–105.

Marx, Karl, and Friedrich Engels (1848). *Manifesto of the Communist Party*.

Maslove, Allan M. (1972). *The Pattern of Taxation in Canada*. Economic Council of Canada (December).

McGillivray, Don (1976). An Over-Simplified Look at Our Complicated Taxes. *Financial Times of Canada* (November 8).

Meerman, Jacob P. (1974). The Definition of Income in Studies of Budget Incidence and Income Distribution. *Review of Income and Wealth* 20, 4 (December): 512–22.

Mencken, H. L. (1989). *A New Dictionary of Quotations on Historical Principles from Ancient and Modern Times*. New York: Alfred A. Knopf.

Mihlar, Fazil (1998). *The Cost of Regulation in Canada, 1998 Edition*. Public Policy Sources 12. Vancouver, BC: The Fraser Institute.

Moroz, Andrew R., and Stephen L. Brown (1987). *Grant Support and Trade Protection for Canadian Industries*. Institute for Research on Public Policy (April).

Musgrave, Richard A., and Peggy B. Musgrave (1973). *Public Finance in Theory and Practice*. McGraw-Hill.

Organisation for Economic Cooperation and Development (1997a). *Agricultural Policies, Markets and Trade: Monitoring and Outlook, 1997*. Paris: OECD.

——— (1997b). *OECD Economic Surveys, Canada, 1997*. Paris: OECD.

——— (1998). *Revenue Statistics 1965–1997*. Paris: OECD.

Pechman, Joseph A., and Benjamin A. Okner (1974). *Who Bears the Tax Burden? Studies of Government Finance.* Washington, DC: The Brookings Institute.

Star, Spencer, and Sally C. Pipes. *Income and Taxation in Canada 1961–1975.* Vancouver, BC: The Fraser Institute.

Tanzi, Vito, and Ludger Schuknecht (1995). *The Growth of Government and the Reform of the State in Industrial Countries.* International Monetary Fund.

Walker, Michael (ed.) (1976). *The Illusion of Wage and Price Control: Essays on Inflation, its Causes and its Cures.* Vancouver, BC: The Fraser Institute.

——— (1978). *Canadian Confederation at the Crossroads: The Search for a Federal-Provincial Balance.* Vancouver, BC: The Fraser Institute.

Watkins, G. Campbell, and Michael A. Walker (eds.) (1977). *Oil in the Seventies.* Vancouver, BC: The Fraser Institute.

Wonnacott, Ronald J., and P. Wonnacott (1967). *Free Trade between the United States and Canada.* Cambridge, MA: Harvard University Press.

The Fraser Institute's series, *Tax Facts*

Walker, Michael, with Sally Pipes, John Raybould, and Spencer Star (1976). *How Much Tax Do You Really Pay? Your Real Tax Guide.*

Pipes, Sally, and Michael Walker (1979). *Tax Facts: The Canadian Consumer Tax Index and You.*

Pipes, Sally, and Michael Walker, with David Gill (1982). *Tax Facts 3: The Canadian Consumer Tax Index and You.*

Pipes, Sally, and Michael Walker, with Douglas Wills (1984). *Tax Facts 4: The Canadian Consumer Tax Index and You.*

——— (1986). *Tax Facts 5: The Canadian Consumer Tax Index and You.*

Pipes, Sally, and Michael Walker, with Isabella Horry (1988). *Tax Facts 6: The Canadian Consumer Tax Index and You.*

Horry, Isabella, Sally Pipes, and Michael Walker (1990). *Tax Facts 7: The Canadian Consumer Tax Index and You.*

Horry, Isabella, Filip Palda, and Michael Walker (1992). *Tax Facts 8.*

——— (1994). *Tax Facts 9.*

Horry, Isabella, Filip Palda, and Michael Walker, with Joel Emes (1997). *Tax Facts 10.*

Government sources

Bank of Canada (various issues). *Bank of Canada Review* (monthly).

Fair Tax Commission, Ontario (1992). *Corporate Minimum Tax* (March).

Department of Finance, Canada (1996). *The Budget Plan* (March 6).

Government of Canada (1867). Constitution Act.

Government of Canada, House of Commons Debates (1917). July 25: 3,765.

Revenue Canada (1995). *Tax Statistics on Individuals, 1993 Tax Year.*

Statistics Canada (various issues). *Canadian Economic Observer.* Cat. 11-010-XPB. Ottawa.

—— (1995). *Agriculture Economic Statistics.* Cat. 21-603e, annual. Ottawa: Supply and Services Canada.

—— *Compendium of Public Sector Statistics.* Ottawa: Supply and Services Canada.

—— (1994). *Federal Government Revenue and Expenditure.* Ottawa: Public Institutions Division.

—— (1995). *Income Distribution by Size in Canada.* Cat. 13-207, annual. Ottawa: Household Surveys Division.

—— (1994). *Local Government Revenue and Expenditure.* Ottawa: Public Institutions Division.

—— (various issues). *National Economic and Financial Accounts.* Cat. 13-001-XPB. Ottawa: National Accounts and Environment Division.

—— (various issues). *National Income and Expenditure Accounts.* Cat. 13-001, quarterly. Ottawa: National Accounts and Environment Division.

—— *Provincial Economic Accounts, Annual Estimates.* Cat. 13-213XD. Ottawa: National Accounts and Environment Division.

—— (1994). *Provincial Government Revenue and Expenditure.* Ottawa: Public Institutions Division.

—— (1992). *Public Finance Historical Data, 1965/66–1991/92.* Cat. 68-512, occasional. Ottawa: Public Institutions Division.

—— (1996). *Public Sector Finance, 1995–1996.* Cat. 68-212-XPB. Ottawa: Public Institutions Division.

—— (1995). *Public Sector Finance, 1994–1995.* Cat. 68-212, annual. Ottawa: Public Institutions Division.

—— (unpublished data). *Survey of Consumer Finances (1994).* Household Surveys Division.